SWU-NAP- 007

UNIFORMS OF RUSSIAN ARMY DURING THE NAPOLEONIC WAR VOL.2

UNDER THE REIGN OF PAUL I
EMPEROR OF RUSSIA BETWEEN 1796 AND 1801
INFANTRY GRENADIERS, MUSKETEERS & JAGERS

From the Viskovatov's greatest work:
"Historical description of the clothing and arms of the Russian Army"

English translation by Mark Conrad

SOLDIERSHOP PUBLISHING

AUTHOR

Aleksandr Vasilevich Viskovatov born 22 April (4 May New Style) 1804, died 27 February (11 March) 1858 in St. Petersburg, Russian military historian. He graduated from the 1st Cadet Corps and served in the artillery, the hydrographic depot of the Naval Ministry, and then in the Department of Military Educational Institutions. He mainly studied historical artifacts and the histories of military units. Viskovatov's greatest work was the Historical Description of the Clothing and Arms of the Russian Army.

TRANSLATOR

Mark Conrad is an American historian with a great interest for all the Russian history.

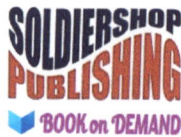

Title: **UNIFORMS OF RUSSIAN ARMY DURING THE NAPOLEONIC WAR VOL. 2-**
The Infantry Grenadiers, Musketeers & Jägers
By A.V.Viskovatov. English translation by Mark Conrad. First edition by Soldiershop.
Cover & Art Design: Luca S. Cristini. Plates re-colorations by Anna Cristini
ISBN code: 978-88-93270502

Published by Soldiershop publishing, via Padre Davide, 7 - 24050 Zanica (BG) ITALY. www.soldiershop.com

UNIFORMS
OF THE RUSSIAN
ARMY DURING THE
NAPOLEONIC WAR VOL.2

UNDER THE REIGN OF PAUL I EMPEROR OF
RUSSIA BETWEEN 1796 AND 1801

*

The Infantry Grenadiers, Musketeers & Jägers

HISTORICAL DESCRIPTION OF THE CLOTHING AND ARMS
OF THE RUSSIAN ARMY - A.V. VISKOVATOV
(First English translation by Mark Conrad)

Soldiershop is glad to presents the complete collection of the great job made by A.V. Viskovatov dedicated to the uniforms and weapons belonging to the Russian army during the Napoleonic period, until 1825. The time we considered corresponds to the reigns of two Tzars: Paul I, who reigned since 1769 until his murder on the 23rd of March 1801, and his son Aleksandr Pavlovi☐ Romanov, that with the title of Alexander I, sat on the throne until the 1st December 1825.

Our reprint in based on the original 19th century volumes, to be precise the volumes from 7 to 9 are dedicated to the reign of Paul I; this first part is distributed on 7 volumes, having a numbering from 1 to 7. From number 10 to 18 of the original volumes, the second part is dedicated to the Russian troops under Alexander I. These still being worked on and they will be soon ready, distributed on twenty volumes approximately. Our new edition, the first ever published in English, both on paper and digital format, boasts a large number of color plates, many of them unpublished and coloured by our team of expert artists and scholars of uniformology. Each volume is based on 50/70 plates, always accompanied by the original translated text which describes the uniforms, the organization and the armament of the Russian army of the period.

A unique work in its genre, a must have in any respecting collection!

Aleksandr Vasilevich Viskovatov born 22 April (4 May New Style) 1804, died 27 February (11 March) 1858 in St. Petersburg, Russian military historian. He graduated from the 1st Cadet Corps and served in the artillery, the hydrographic depot of the Naval Ministry, and then in the Department of Military Educational Institutions.

He mainly studied historical artifacts and the histories of military units. Viskovatov's greatest work was the Historical Description of the Clothing and Arms of the Russian Army (Vols. 1-30, St. Petersburg, 1841-62; 2nd ed. Vols. 1-34, St. Petersburg - Novosibirsk - Leningrad, 1899-1948). This work is based on a great quantity of archival documents and contains four thousand colored illustrations.

Viskovatov was the author of Chronicles of the Russian Army (Books 1-20, St. Petersburg, 1834-42) and Chronicles of the Russian Imperial Army (Parts 1-7, St. Petersburg, 1852). He collected valuable material on the history of the Russian navy which went into A Short Overview of Russian Naval Campaigns and General Voyages to the End of the XVII Century (St. Petersburg, 1864; 2nd edition Moscow, 1946). Together with A.I. Mikhailovskii-Danilevskii he helped prepare and create the Military Gallery in the Winter Palace.

He wrote the historical military inscriptions for the walls of the Hall of St. George in the Great Palace of the Kremlin. (From the article in the Soviet Military Encyclopedia.)

CONTENTS

*

Preface pag. 5

*

Field, or army infantry 1796 -1801 pag. 7

*

Notes pag. 34

*

PLATES pag. 41

FIELD, OR ARMY, INFANTRY 1796-1801

Changes in the uniforms and equipment of the Field, or Army, Infantry from 1796 to 1801
I. Grenadier regiments
II. Musketeer regiments
III. Jäger regiments

In regard to uniforms and weapons, EMPEROR PAUL I made the following changes and innovations:

I. FIELD, OR ARMY, GRENADIER REGIMENTS (*Polevye ili Armeiskie Grenaderskie polki*)

29 November 1796 – With the issue of a new set of Military Regulations (*Voinskii Ustav*), the clothing, weapons, and accouterments of Grenadier regiments were prescribed to be almost the same as for the Gatchina troops described above. Following these Regulations and later directives with only insignificant deviations, HIGHEST confirmed authorization tables (*shtaty*) of 5 January 1798 laid down the full uniform clothing of a private fusilier (*ryadovoi fuzeler*) as: coat, waistcoat, breeches, gaiters, shoes, neck cloth, fusilier cap, forage cap, greatcoat, and, for winter, a warm coat. Weapons and accouterment items included: sword with sword knot, waistbelt with bayonet frog, musket with bayonet, musket sling, firelock cover and frizzen cover, cartridge pouch with belt, knapsack with strap, water flask, and rusk bag (Illus. Nos. 912-919) (168).

Coat (*kaftan*, also called *mundir*)-of dark-green soaked cloth (*mochenoe sukno*), with red kersey (*karazeinyi*) lining and flat metal buttons (brass or tin), in cut almost exactly the same as the coats of the Gatchina infantry. For most of the regiments it had lapels (*otvoroty* or *latskany*) and lace loops (*nashivki* or *petlitsy*). The lace loops were of wool tape and only on the cuff flaps above the cuffs, except for the Moscow Regiment in which they were on the cuffs themselves running straight from the upper edge to the lower. As in the Gatchina force, the collar was sewn flat to the coat and about 2-1/4 vershoks (4 inches) wide. The lapels had almost the same form as for Army infantry under EMPRESS CATHERINE II except for being a little wider at the top. Also, since the collar edge was about four fingers width from the coat's front opening, there was a triangular piece of dark-green cloth that showed between the collar's side, the top of the lapel, and the upper edge of the coat (Illus. Nos. 912, 913, and 914). Each lapel fastened to the coat with six buttons, of which the lower five, sewn directly to the coat, were equally spaced while the top button was sewn to the collar at the shoulder and was further away. One more button was on the collar on the left side, for attaching the shoulder strap. Two buttons were under the right lapel along the coat's opening. Two were above each cuff on the flaps, and three each were on the pocket flaps. Two were at the waist in the back, one was at each of the lower ends of the skirts at the seam, and one was at each of the skirt's fastenings (*po odnoi—u nizhnikh kontsev pol, na shve, in po odnoi—u zastezhek pol*). Coats without lapels had buttons arranged in the same way except that there were five buttons along each side of the front opening instead of six, beginning from the corner of the collar and going to the waist (Illus. No. 915). On these coats, i.e. those without lapels, the front edge of the skirt was cut away with a step as for Gatchina infantry coats in 1793 (Illus. No. 915), while this was absent on coats with lapels. In regard to the coat, regiments were distinguished from one another by the color of the collar, cuffs, lapels, shoulder strap, lace loops, and buttons, a description of which is laid out below. In spring, from 1 March to 1 May, the coat was closed by hooks, and if provided with lapels, then also with the two lower buttons of the right side so that the lapels were still open (Illus. No. 912). In summer, from 1 May to 1 September, the coat was closed only by the middle hooks opposite the third and fourth buttons from the bottom (Illus. No. 913). In fall, from 1 September to 1 November, it was closed using all the buttons except the two at the bottom (Illus. No. 914), and in winter, from 1 November to 1 March—using all buttons without exception (Illus. No. 915) (169).

Waistcoat (kamzol)—white in some regiments, of pale straw color in others, and in still others—of lemon yellow (*tsitronnyi*) cloth. As before, it was lined with linen, reached below the waist, had flaps on the pockets, and small flat buttons. These buttons were the same color as those on the coat and sewn along the front opening (ten) and on the pocket flaps (two each). In the cold months of the year waistcoats were worn with sleeves, but in summer these were unstitched and removed (170).

Breeches (shtany)—also called underclothes (*nizhee plat'e*)—of the same pattern as infantry breeches up to 1786, i.e. the uniform changes introduced in the Russian army by Prince Potemkin. From 1 June to 1 September they were white linen, and in the remaining months of cloth the same color as the waistcoat (171).

Gaiters (shtiblety)—of black cloth with twelve yellow buttons on each side, the same size and shape as those on the waistcoat. Gaiters were fastened under the third button from the top by a black cloth strap (*podvyazka*) with a rectangular buckle, rounded at the corners, and were exactly like the gaiters used by Gatchina infantry (Illus. No. 912) (172).

Shoes (bashmaki)—greased, with blunt toes (173).

Neck cloth (galstuk)—made from red stamin (*stamed*), lined and trimmed with linen on the upper edge, with tape or ribbons at the back (174).

Fusilier cap (fuzelernaya shapka)—similar to the caps used by the Gatchina Artillery and described above in the survey of EMPEROR PETER III's reign. It consisted of a cloth crown, a band, and a front piece. The latter, 5-1/2 vershoks (9-5/8 inches) high, had, on the outer side over its whole height, a metal (the same color as the buttons) plate on which there was a crown at the top and below that the Cyrillic inscription: "*S nami Bog*" ("*God is with us*"). Below the inscription-a two-headed eagle above the monogram of EMPEROR PAUL I formed from the Cyrillic letter P and the numeral I. The remaining space within the plate was taken up by a martial armature and other designs (Illus. No. 916). Bent over the crown were two crossed metal *strips (poloski)*, convex and decorated with tracings. Where the strips crossed was a convex cap or little hat (*kolpachek*), likewise of metal, with a decorative flame on top. On the band opposite the strips were fixed three metal plates each with the depiction of a flaming grenade and various tracings (Illus. No. 916) (175).

Forage cap (furazhnaya shapka)—with or without a band, similar to the usual cap (*kolpak*) and made from dark-green cloth, namely the remnants of worn-out coats. It was bent at the midpoint of its length or height, and had a woolen tassel hanging down below whose lower end was even with the lower end of the cap itself (i.e. the upper edge of the band - M.C.) (Illus. No. 197). The color of the band varied, but for the most part was the same as the collar, lapels, and cuffs. The tassel likewise had no prescribed color, and care was only taken that it was different for each of the companies within a battalion. In some regiments there was decorative cloth piping along the cap's seams, of no determined color. Also in some regiments, the part of the cap from the bend to the tassel was longer than from the bend to the bottom of the band, and in such cases the first, long, part began its bend so that the end of the tassel was even with the lower edge of the band (Illus. No. 917) (176).

Greatcoat (shinel')—of white cloth, without lining, similar to the cloaks (*plashchi*) previously introduced by Prince Potemkin except it had a fold-down collar like that on the coat, and six covered buttons (Illus. No. 914) (177). It was worn in cold or inclement weather over the *kaftan* coat with arms in the sleeves, girded with a sword belt (*podpoyasyvaya portupeeyu*). During weather when it was not needed, it was carried rolled or tied to the top of the knapsack, or thrown back over the shoulder, however was found convenient (178).

Warm coat (fufaika)—this was the term for a sheepskin coat (*ovchinnyi polushubok*) worn from 1 November to 1 March under the waistcoat, for which the latter had a string at the back let out, and the *kaftan* coat let out its extra material expressly provided for this purpose (179).

With this uniform clothing powder, curls, and queues (*pudra, pukli i kosy*) were reintroduced. The second of these were worn to be a palm's breadth wide and long enough to cover the ears, and the last of these were plaited with a black woolen tape tied at the nape of the neck with a bow with two small ends. The length of the queue itself was not defined, but for uniformity regimental *Chefs* saw to it that its lower end was even with the upper edge of the cartridge pouch (180). When not on duty, privates were allowed to wear their hair in a club (*puchka*) instead of a queue (181).

Sword (shpaga)—with a short-sword blade (*tesachnyi klinok*), 15 vershoks (26-1/4 inches) long. It had a scabbard of unblackened leather, while the hilt, hook (for hanging it in the frog on the sword belt), and end piece were brass, and was almost exactly like the swords from the time of EMPEROR PETER III (Illus. No. 918) (182). The sword knot (*shpazhnyi temlyak*) consisted of a woolen strap 5/8 vershok (1-1/10 inch) wide, a similarly woolen tassel which including the knot (*stolbchik*, literally "little column" - M.C.) and loop (*gaika*), or *shisheshka* (literally "small pine cone" - M.C.), was 2-1/2 vershoks (4-3/8 inches) long (Illus. 918). The strap and tassel fringe were white. The knots were white in the 1st battalions and red in the 2nd, while the loop and upper ring (*okolysh*, the upper rounded part of the tassel) were white in the 1st or *Chef's* company, orange in the 2nd, black in the 3rd, sky blue in the 4th, and red in the 5th (183).

Sword belt (portupeya)—of whitened leather from cows that have not yet calved (*yalovochnaya kozha*), with stitching along the edges and a sewn frog. It was prescribed to be 1 arshin 13 vershoks (50-3/4 inches) long, and, as before, 1-1/8 vershoks (2 inches) wide. At its lower edge, between the straps that formed a frog (*lopast'*) for the sword, was sewn a smaller frog for the bayonet scabbard. From the back of the right end, almost opposite the waistcoat opening, was attached a narrow strap to pass through a small brass or iron buckle sewn to the left end's front side (Illus. 918). When the sword belt was fastened in this manner, the brass rectangular buckle on it was moved leftward from the right side until its middle was opposite the waistcoat button, and the long end of the sword belt that then remained was passed through a loop made from a strap sewn between the sword frog's front strap and the bayonet frog. Then, the same end of the sword belt, by means of a small iron hook sewn onto it, was held by a small iron loop sewn on the front side of the belt at such a distance from the end that the entire strap lay along the man's waist as flat as possible. In summer uniform, i.e. when only the upper hooks on the *kaftan* coat were fastened, the sword belt was worn over the waist coat so that the sword was directly at the side, in front of the left coat skirt. In fall, the sword belt was again worn over the waistcoat, but the frog was put next to the slit in the left skirt so that the sword was almost directly in back, while in winter and spring the belt was worn over the coat (184). The bayonet scabbard (*shtykovyya nozhny*) on the sword belt was about 9 vershoks (15-3/4 inches) long, conforming to the bayonet itself, and made from unblackened leather, with a brass hook and end piece (185).

Musket (ruzh'e)—of Prussian pattern, with a ramrod, bayonet, brass mountings, and a hazel-wood stock. Without the bayonet it was 1 arshin 14-1/2 vershoks (53-3/8 inches) long, and with the bayonet—2 arshins 7 vershoks (68-1/4 inches) (Illus. No. 918). —The *musket sling (ruzheinyi remen')* was passed through a ring: one end opposite the middle of the ramrod and the other at the butt under the bracket. It was made from red Russian leather, and its upper surface was painted red and then lacquered (186). —The *firelock cover (ognivnyi chekhol)* was of the same kind of leather as the sling and painted in the same manner. It was always in place except when actually firing (187).

Frizzen cover (polunagalishche)—likewise of red Russian leather, 7-1/2 vershoks (13-1/8 inches) long, 3 vershoks (5-1/4 inches) wide in the middle, and 2 vershoks (3-1/2 inches) wide at the ends. It was fastened with four small leather buttons which corresponded to the same number of loops (Illus. 918) (188).

Cartridge pouch (patronnaya suma)—on the outside of blackened polished leather, and unblackened on the inside. It was trimmed along its edges with a narrow strip of red Russian leather and on the cover had a round brass badge with the image of a two-headed eagle (Illus. 918) (189). The length of the cover along its upper edge was 6-1/2 vershoks (11-3/8 inches), its width in the center was 6 vershoks (10-1/2 inches), the length of the pouch itself—5-1/2 vershoks (9-5/8 inches), its width—1-3/4 vershoks (3 inches), and its depth—3-1/4 vershoks (5-5/8 inches). —*Cross belt (perevyaz')*, attached by a buckle sewn to the lower side of the pouch, made of leather from cows that have not yet calved and prescribed to be: length—2 arshins 3 vershoks (5 feet 1-1/4 inches), width—2-1/8 vershoks (3-3/4 inches). Like the sword belt, it was stitched along the edges and whitened, and fastened to the pouch so that the latter's upper edge was almost even with the right hand button at the waist (190).

Knapsack (ranets)—this was a special article for campaign use. It was four-sided and made from calfskin with the hair on the outside, without lining. Its width along the upper edge was 9-3/4 vershoks (17-1/16 inches), its height—about 7 vershoks (12-1/4 inches), and its depth—about 2 vershoks (3-1/2 inches). On its outside, for closing the flap or cover, there were three iron buckles, and on the sides along the upper edge—two more. The latter served to fasten a strap which had no prescribed width and was cut from worn-out cross belts. The knapsack was worn over the right shoulder on top of the cross belt, taking care that it was even with cartridge pouch (Illus. No. 919) (191).

Water flask (vodonosnaya flyazha)—of doubled tin, it was, without its cover, 3-5/8 vershoks (6-1/3 inches) tall, and with its cover—4-1/2 vershoks (7-7/8 inches). It was 3-3/4 vershoks (6-5/8 inches) wide in front and 1-3/4 vershoks (3-1/16 inches) wide at the sides. It was held to the knapsack by a white strap that, like the knapsack strap, was cut from worn-out cross belts and sword belts (Illus. 919) (192).

Bag for rusk (sukharnyi meshok)—a campaign article like the previous two items, and almost always referred to as a *lakomka* ("treats bag"). It was a plain leather bag about 8-1/2 vershoks (14-7/8 inches) long, 7 vershoks (12-1/4 inches) wide, and 3/4 vershok (5/8 inch) thick, with two iron buckles at the upper ends (Illus. 919) (193). The ends of a strap were passed through these buckles, and the strap was worn over the waistcoat across the left shoulder so that the bag itself was under the coat's right skirt (194). Later this bag came to be worn for a time over the coat, under the knapsack. —The leather used for rusk bags could be either black or white according to the decision of the Regimental *Chef*, observing only that there was not parti-colored variation within a regiment (195).

Non-commissioned officers in Fusilier companies—differed from private fusiliers in regard to uniform clothing in that they had gold or silver galloon (according to the color of the buttons) on the edges of the collar and cuffs, about 1/2 vershok (7/8 inch) in width. Exactly the same galloon was also sewn above the cuffs along two edges of the flaps: the upper edge and that side where the buttons were (Illus. 920). Following the example of the Prussian army, non-commissioned officers were prescribed chamois *gloves (zamshevyya perchatki)* with flaps, or cuffs, colored with ocher to match the waistcoat, and reed *canes (kamyshevyya trosti)* with a wide top piece (*nabaldashnik*) of white bone and an equally wide brass end piece, and with a knot of unblackened leather passing through below the top piece. When in formation, the cane was hung by its knot to the second (third if there were lapels) button from the top on the left side of the coat, and the cane's lower end was put between the top of the left skirt and its turnback (196). Muskets, cartridge pouches, and cross belts were not authorized for fusilier non-commissioned officers, and they had—except for the non-commissioned officers with the company flag—halberds (*gallebardy* or *albardy*). These had three rounded points on each side. The iron head or "feather" was 5-1/2 vershoks (9-5/8 inches) long, the socket 2-3/4 vershoks (4-7/8 inches) long, and the shaft with the butt piece 2 arshins 14-1/2 vershoks (81-3/4 inches) long (Illus. No. 920) (197). The last was painted the color of straw (*palevyi*) in the first two regiments of a division and black in the rest of the regiments. For non-commissioned officers the sword, sword belt, knapsack, water flask, and rusk bag were the same as for privates, except that the second had no frog for a bayonet scabbard, and the sword knot had black and orange silk within the tassel and on its ring (*okolysh*). The remaining parts of the sword knot were of the same colors as for privates.

Drummers in fusilier companies (barabanshchiki Fuzelernykh rot) had the same uniforms as fusiliers except that their coats had: 1) small swallows' nests (*kryl'tsy*) on the shoulders of the same color as the collar, lapels, and cuffs; 2) four cross stripes sewn on the front half of the sleeve, of the exact same tape as used for buttonholes on the cuff flaps, and 3) a shoulder strap not on the left, but the right shoulder (Illus. No. 920). Drummers were not authorized muskets, cartridge pouches, or cross belts, and instead had a drum (*baraban*) with its cross belt (*perevyaz'*) and an apron (*zanaveska*). —The first was made of copper brass (*mednyi latun'*) as before, with the raised image of a two-headed eagle inside an oval, two wooden hoops or frames, and cords with whitened leather tabs. It was 9-1/2 vershoks (16-5/8 inches) high (including the hoops) and the same in diameter. The inside of the hoops were painted white, and the outside had triangular teeth in two colors: dark green and the same color as prescribed for the regiment's collar, lapels, and cuffs. Care was taken that the dark-green triangles pointed toward the brass of the drum (Illus. No. 921) (198). —*Drum belt (perevyaz' barabannaya)*—2-1/2 vershoks (3-3/4 inches) wide, made of leather from cows that had not yet calved, whitened and stitched the same as cartridge-pouch cross belts. It was fastened behind by a brass buckle and had an end piece, also of brass. A narrow strap was fixed to its lower edge from which the drum was hung, and on the front side, opposite the center of the chest, were sewn whitened leather loops for the drumsticks. The last were 10 vershoks (17-1/2 inches) long with brass mountings on the upper ends, and painted the same color as halberd shafts (199). —*Aprons (zanaveski)* for the drums were, as before, made from calfskin with the hair side facing out, of uniform color (200).

Privates in Grenadier companies were distinguished from fusiliers only in having sword knots with green loops and rings (*gaiki i okolyshi*) on the tassels (201), four flaming grenades at the corners of the cartridge pouch's cover (202), and a different headdress (Illus. No. 922). The last was exactly as for Gatchina Grenadiers but with a plate and grenades the same color as the buttons, a rear section the same color as prescribed for a regiment's collar, lapels, and cuffs, and for the most part, a dark-green band. There was no prescribed color for the trim on the rear section but in most cases it was yellow with black or dark-green cross stripes. At the top the tassel itself was of black and yellow wool. In those regiments in which the *Chef* was a member of the Royal Family (*VYSOCHAISHAYA OSOBA*), the image of the *Keizer-flag* below the plate was prescribed to be of finift enamel, but it all other cases it was to be unpainted (203).

Non-commissioned officers in Grenadier companies were uniformed similarly to private grenadiers but with the addition of galloon lace, gloves, and canes, as related above for non-commissioned officers in Fusilier companies, and with the same sword-knot distinctions as described above. Their weapons were the same as for private grenadiers except their muskets were rifled (*ruzh'ya vintoval'nyya*), and instead of cartridge pouches they had small pouches (*podsumki*) called *patrontashi* (from German *Patronentasche* - M.C.). These were of polished black leather with the same round badge as on the cartridge pouch, and were worn in front on the sword belt (Illus. No. 922) (204).

Drummers in Grenadier companies were uniformed and armed the same as grenadiers, with the distinctions noted above for drummers in Fusilier companies (Illus. No. 923) (205).

Fifers (fleishchiki) in Grenadier companies were distinguished from drummers only in having a shoulder strap on the left shoulder instead of the right. Of the weapons and accouterments carried by drummers, they were not prescribed the drum, carrying belt, and apron, but over the left shoulder they wore a brass carrying case (*futlyar*) on a strap made from the whitened leather of a cow that had not yet calved. This case had two fifes almost the same in appearance as those used today in the reign of Nicholas Pavlovich (Illus. No. 923) (206).

Regimental drummer—prescribed to be of non-commissioned officer rank, he had the exact same uniform, gloves, and cane as non-commissioned officers in Fusilier companies except that in addition to the sewn-on stripes on his coat, as authorized for company drummers, similar lace was on all seams and also along the lower edge of the swallows' nests (Illus. No. 924). His weapons and accouterments, including a drum, carrying strap, and apron, were the same as for company drummers (Illus. No. 924) (207).

Regimental musicians, namely: 2 clarinet players (*klarnetisty*), 2 Waldhornists (*voltornisty*), and 1 hautboy players (*goboist*), were all uniformed and armed after the example of a regimental drummer but without the shoulder strap, gloves, or cane (Illus. No. 925) (208).

Company-grade officers (ober-ofitsery) of both Fusilier and Grenadier companies, wore: a *coat*, *waistcoat*, winter and summer *breeches*, *gaiters*, and *shoes*, of the same patterns and colors as for lower combatant ranks, except that the first had no shoulder strap but rather gold and silver buttonhole loops, with gold or silver buttons, and was lined with unpolished stamin (*neloshchenyi stamed*), the skirts not being turned back. There was also a difference in the number and positioning of the buttons since for officers' coats with lapels there were seven buttons on each side, and six without lapels. The buttons were sewn on in pairs or couples (*poparno ili gnezdami*) and were raised and convex (Illus. No. 926) (209). Like non-commissioned officers, company-grade officers wore gloves with cuffs, and canes. The first were the same color as the waistcoat and the latter were only carried when not in formation. Officers wore neck cloths which were—except those in the Moscow Regiment which were of black serge—of fine quality white canvas (*kanifas*) folded four or five times according to the neck size, and tied in back. All officers without exception had hats (*shlyapy*) which were almost the same size and shape as those during the reign of EMPEROR PETER III. In the Moscow Regiment hats had wide toothed galloon while other regiments had narrow flat-edged galloon, gold or silver according to the color of the buttons. At each side corner of the hat was a tassel of gold with black silk, to each of which were fastened the ends of the same cord that circled the crown one time. A short time later in regiments with white distinctions, and later in all regiments without exception, these tassels as well as the cord were silver mixed with black and orange (210). Hat trimmed with wide galloon had on the left brim a bow or cockade of black silk ribbon with orange edges, a wide buttonhole loop of smooth gold or silver cord with an eight-pointed star on the upper part, and below the buttonhole—a button of the same color (Illus. No. 927) (211). In the last years of EMPEROR PAUL I's reign similar cockades and buttonhole loops were given to all officers' hats without exception, but before that time narrow galloon was accompanied only by tassels with a cord and one button (Illus. No. 929) (212). When wearing this uniform, company-grade officers wore a sword with sword knot and sword belt, when on duty—a sash, and when in full formation dress or parade uniform (*polnaya stroevaya, ili paradnaya forma*)—a gorget and spontoon were added.

The *sword (shpaga)* had a gilt hilt with rounded cups on the front as well as on the opposite side. The grip was wrapped with gold wire, and the scabbard was of unblackened leather on which the hook and end piece were also gilded (Illus. No. 928). The sword was carried on a deerskin or chamois (*losinnaya ili zamshevaya*) sword belt of a color similar to that of the waistcoat. The sword belt was worn under the waistcoat: in summer—under the left skirt, and at other times—further back towards the rear opening of the skirt tails (213).

Sword knot (temlyak)—silver with two rows of black and orange silk along the edges of the lace strap. A similar mixture of silk was in the ring (*gaika*), knot (*stolbchik*), and the interior of the tassel within the fringe (Illus. No. 928) (214).

Sash (sharf)—also silver, with stripes of black and orange silk that, as in the sword knot, were also found in the center of the tassels (Illus. 928). In summer uniform the sash was worn around the waistcoat, and at other times of the year—over the coat, tying the tassels on the left side in front of the sword (215).

Gorget (znak)—of silver or just covered with silver, on a ribbon of black silk with an orange edge. Its edge was lined with turned up reinforcement, and its center was decorated with a gilt armature forming an oval, with a crown at the top and a black two-headed eagle within, on straw-colored enamel (*na palevoi finifti*) (Illus. No. 928) (216).

Spontoon (espanton)—with a blade (*pero*) 6 vershoks (10-1/2 inches) long, an iron cross piece (*zheleztso*) 3-1/4 vershoks (5-5/8 inches) long, a socket 2-3/4 vershoks (4-7/8 inches) long, and a shaft with butt piece 2 arshins 14-1/2 vershoks (81-3/8 inches) long. It was of almost the same pattern as the spontoons introduced by EMPEROR PETER III, but the blade, instead of having a gold cut-out, had the engraved image of a two-headed eagle within which was the HIGHEST monogram of the Cyrillic letter P and number I, with the name of the regiment below. The shaft was the same color as those of the regiment's halberds (Illus. No. 928) (217).

The *Chef's Adjutant (Shefskii Ad"yutant)* and the *Regimental Adjutant (Polkovyi Ad"yutant)* had the same uniforms and weapons as other company-grade officers but did not have spontoons. They always wore boots (*sapogi*) with bell tops and steel or silver spurs fastened above the heel with the help of a piece of leather (*nadshpornik*) and buckle the same color as the spur, along with a leather strap below (*podshpornik*). These boots were always to be worn with gaiter cuffs (*shtibel'-manzhety*), and the coat's skirts were turned up. All straps of Adjutants' horse furniture (*konskii ubor*) along with their pistol holsters (*ol'stry*) were black. The (English) saddle (*sedlo*) was likewise black, with a narrow brass strip along the rear arch. Pistols (*pistolety*) had brass mountings, while the saddlecloth (*cheprak*) and pistol carriers (*chushki*) were of dark-green cloth with gold or silver galloon (according to the color of the buttons) about 3/4 vershok (1-3/8 inches) wide, with sharp corners, of almost the same pattern as the saddlecloths and pistol carriers used by infantry officers up to the present (the reign of EMPEROR NICHOLAS PAVLOVICH) (Illus. No. 929) (218).

Field-grade officers (shtab-ofitsery), when in parade dress, had nothing to distinguish them from company-grade officers, and when mounted appeared the same as Adjutants. However, when not on duty they always wore boots with spurs, gaiter cuffs, and a coat with the tails turned back (219).

Generals (generaly) commanding regiments, or who were their *Chefs*, were distinguished from field-grade officers only in having hats with wide, toothed galloon, a cockade, buttonhole loop, and white plumage trim (*plyumazh*) (Illus. No. 931) (220).

All officers and generals powdered and styled their hair into *curls* and a *queue* braided with a black silk ribbon, and when not in formation they could wear dark-green *frock coats (sertuki)* lined with red unpolished stamin in summer and with red kersey in winter. The pattern for these frock coats was the same as for *kaftan* coats without lapels, except that they were made more simply. The collar, cuffs, and buttons were of the colors prescribed for the regiment (221). Besides the frock these ranks also had greatcoats (*shineli*) of dark-green cloth, with six covered buttons in front and two collars: a standing one about 3/4 vershok (1-3/8 inches) high and another lying down about 5-1/4 inches wide (Illus. No. 933) (222).

Noncombatant lower ranks (nestroevye nizhnie chiny), such as: *chaplain's assistants (tserkovniki)*, *medics (podlekarya* or *fel'dshery)*, *barbers (tsiryul'niki)*, *master craftsmen (masterovye)*, *gunstock craftsmen (lozhniki), metal workers (slesarya), provosts (profosy), train personnel (pogonshchiki or furleity)*, were prescribed a *frock coat, waistcoat, breeches, boots, neckcloth, hat* (Illus. No. 934), *forage cap, greatcoat*; for winter a *warm coat (fufaika), knapsack, water flask*, and *rusk bag*.

Frock coat (sertuk)—reaching to the calf (*podvyazok*, or "garter"), of dark-green cloth, with two rows of buttons,. One standing collar and another lying down, round cuffs, also dark green. Lining of red kersey, flat buttons of the regimental color, seven on each side of the front opening and always fastened (223).

Waistcoat and *breeches (kamzol i shtany)* were of the same pattern as for combatant ranks: the first of dark-green cloth with similarly covered buttons, and the second—white, linen in summer and of cloth the rest of the time (224).

Boots—with blunt toes, reaching to the knee (225).

Neck cloth, hat, forage cap, greatcoat, knapsack, water flask, and *rusk bag*—also of the patterns used by combatant ranks, except that the first was dark green and the second had no ornamentation or trim apart from a draw cord and button (226).

Noncombatant officials of officer rank, such as: *Quartermaster, Legal Assistant*, and *Doctor*—had the following uniform clothing:

Quartermaster (Kvartermistr)—dark-green *kaftan* coat without lapels, with likewise dark-green falling collar, slit cuffs with two buttons, white (silvered) buttons, and lining of red unpolished stamin; dark-green waistcoat with silver buttons and likewise silver galloon; straw-colored breeches, boots with bell tops and spurs; gaiter cuffs; black neck cloth; officer's pattern hat as worn in the Moscow Grenadier Regiment except with entirely silver tassels; gloves with gauntlet cuffs; cane and officer's sword with silver sword knot without any colored silk (Illus. No. 935).

Legal Assistant (Auditor)—all as for the Quartermaster, but the hat without tassels and the sword without a sword knot (Illus. 935).

Doctor (Lekar')—the same as the Legal Assistant but with green lining to the coat (Illus. No. 935) (227).

In regard to colors, uniforms, and weapons, Grenadier regiments had the following distinctions:

In the Yekaterinoslav Regiment, later renamed the *Pskov Regiment*:

Lower ranks—coat without collar or lapels, with yellow cuffs and shoulder strap; white buttonhole loops on the sleeves, without small tassels; straw-colored waistcoat and breeches; yellow buttons; yellow back piece and band on the cap; trim on grenadier caps-red with black (Illus. 912); halberd shafts and drumsticks straw colored; drum hoops—dark-green with yellow. *Officers*—gold buttonhole loops on the sleeves, without embroidered thread work (*bez biti*); spontoon shafts straw colored (228).

In the St.-Petersburg Regiment:

Lower ranks—coat without lapels and with rose-colored (*rozovye*) collar, cuffs, and shoulder strap; white buttonhole loops on the sleeves, with rose-colored tracery and small tassels; straw-colored waistcoat and breeches; white buttons; rose-colored back piece and straw-colored (*palevyi*) band on the cap (Illus. No. 913); trim on grenadier caps-yellow with black; halberd shafts and drumsticks straw colored; drum hoops—dark-green with rose. *Officers*—silver buttonhole loops, with rose-colored silk and small tassels; spontoon shafts straw colored (229).

In the Astrakhan Regiment: Lower ranks—coat with apricot-colored (*abrikosovye*) collar, lapels, cuffs, and shoulder strap; white buttonhole loops on the sleeves, with small tassels; white waistcoat and breeches; white buttons; apricot-colored back piece and dark-green band on the cap (Illus. No. 914); trim on grenadier caps—yellow with black; halberd shafts and drumsticks straw colored; drum hoops—dark-green with apricot. *Officers*—silver buttonhole loops, embroidered; spontoon shafts straw colored (230).

In the Kiev Regiment: Lower ranks—coat without color or lapels, scarlet (*alye*) shoulder strap and cuffs; yellow buttonhole loops on the sleeves, without small tassels; straw-colored waistcoat and breeches; yellow buttons; scarlet back piece and dark-green band on the cap; trim on grenadier caps—yellow with black (Illus. No. 915); halberd shafts and drumsticks straw colored; drum hoops—dark-green with scarlet. *Officers*—gold buttonhole loops; spontoon shafts straw colored (231).

In the Little-Russia (Malorossiiskii) Regiment: Lower ranks—coat with light sky-blue (*svelto-golubye*) collar, lapels, and shoulder strap; yellow buttonhole loops on the sleeves, without small tassels; straw-colored waistcoat and breeches; yellow buttons; light sky-blue back piece and dark-green band on the cap; trim on grenadier caps—yellow with black; halberd shafts and drumsticks straw colored; drum hoops—dark-green with light sky-blue (Illus. No. 920). *Officers*—gold buttonhole loops, without small tassels; spontoon shafts straw colored (232).

In the Siberia Regiment: Lower ranks—coat with orange (*oranzhevyi*) collar, lapels, cuffs, and shoulder strap; red buttonhole loops on the sleeves, with small white tassels; white waistcoat and breeches; yellow buttons; orange back piece and dark-green band on the cap; trim on grenadier caps—yellow with black (Illus. No. 922); halberd shafts and drumsticks straw colored; drum hoops—dark-green with orange. *Officers*—gold buttonhole loops, without small tassels; spontoon shafts straw colored (233).

In the Phanagoria Regiment: Lower ranks—coat with iron (*zheleznyi*) collar, lapels, cuffs, and shoulder strap; buttonhole loops on the sleeves with two black stripes, and between the stripe—a black worm (*zmeika*, i.e. zigzag), with small white and black tassels; white waistcoat and breeches; white buttons; light-iron back piece and dark-green band on the cap (Illus. No. 923); trim on grenadier caps—yellow with black; halberd shafts and drumsticks straw colored; drum hoops—colored dark-green and iron. *Officers*—silver buttonhole loops, with small tassels and with black silk mixed in, of the same appearance as for lower ranks; spontoon shafts straw colored (234).

In the Kherson Regiment:

Lower ranks—coat with light-violet (*svetlo-fioletovyi*) collar, cuffs, and shoulder strap; white buttonhole loops on the sleeves, with violet stripes and small tassels of these same two colors; straw-colored waistcoat and breeches; white buttons; light-violet back piece and dark-green band on the cap; trim on grenadier caps—yellow with black; halberd shafts and drumsticks straw colored; drum hoops—black with violet (Illus. No. 924). *Officers*—silver buttonhole loops with violet silk, of the same appearance as for lower ranks; spontoon shafts straw colored (235).

In the Caucasus Regiment:

Lower ranks—coat with chestnut-colored (*kashtanovyi*) collar, lapels, cuffs, and shoulder strap; white buttonhole loops on the sleeves, with two stripes and with small tassels; white waistcoat and breeches; white buttons; dark-chestnut back piece and dark-green band on the cap (Illus. No. 925); trim on grenadier caps—yellow with black; halberd shafts and drumsticks straw colored; drum hoops—black with chestnut. Officers—silver buttonhole loops with two stripes of flattened wire thread (*bit'*), and with small tassels of twisted cord; spontoon shafts straw colored (236).

In the Moscow Regiment:
Lower ranks—coat with brick-red (*krasno-kirpichnyi*) collar, lapels, slit cuffs, and shoulder strap; white buttonhole loops on the cuffs; lemon-colored (*tsitronnyi*) waistcoat and breeches; black neckcloth; white buttons; cherry-colored (*vishnevyi*) back piece and lemon-colored band on the cap; trim on grenadier caps—yellow with black (Illus. No. 926); halberd shafts and drumsticks straw colored; drum hoops-dark—green with brick-red. Officers—silver buttonhole loops on the cuffs; black neckcloth; wide galloon on the hat, with indentations (*gorodki*), bow of black ribbon with orange edges, and a silver buttonhole loop (Illus. No. 926); spontoon shafts straw colored (237).

In the Taurica Regiment:
Lower ranks—coat with orange collar, cuffs, lapels, and shoulder strap; white buttonhole loops on the sleeves, with small tassels; white waistcoat and breeches; white buttons; orange back piece to the cap; trim on grenadier caps—yellow with black, and a dark-green band (Illus. 929); halberd shafts and drumsticks straw colored; drum hoops—dark-green with orange. Officers—silver buttonhole loops, embroidered; spontoon shafts straw colored (Illus. No. 929). In this regiment fusilier caps were made somewhat differently than in the preceding regiments, namely: they were lower and, toward the top, more rounded, and the front piece (4-1/2 vershoks (7-7/8 inches) high) had a plate with an eagle almost entirely covering it (Illus. 930) (238).

In the Pavlovsk Regiment:
Lower ranks—coat with orange collar, lapels, cuffs, and shoulder strap; yellow buttonhole loops on the sleeves, without small tassels; white waistcoat and breeches; yellow buttons; orange back piece and dark-green band on the cap; trim on grenadier caps—yellow with black (Illus. No. 931); halberd shafts and drumsticks straw colored; drum hoops—dark-green with orange. *Officers*—gold buttonhole loops with flattened wire thread, without small tassels (Illus. No. 931); spontoon shafts straw colored. This regiment was distinct from all other Russian Army infantry regiments in that its lower ranks had saber-style hilts (*yefesy sabel'nye*) to their short swords, without cups, and in that on grenadier cap plates the eagle was bigger and colored black (Illus. No. 932) (239).

In the Leib-Grenadier Regiment:
Lower ranks—coat with scarlet collar, cuffs, and shoulder strap; gold galloon buttonhole loops on the sleeves, without small tassels; white waistcoat and breeches; yellow buttons; in Grenadier companies—scarlet back piece and band to the cap, and for Wing companies—yellow back piece and red band; trim on caps—yellow with black (Illus. No. 933); straw-colored halberd and drumsticks; drum hoops—dark-green with red. For *officers*—gold buttonhole loops, without small tassels; straw colored spontoon shafts. This regiment kept the aiguillettes (*aksel'banty*) that it was given in the previous reign. These were worn on the right shoulder, as previously, and for lower ranks were of yellow worsted (*garus*) while for officers they were gold. Further distinctions for this regiment that set it apart from other Army regiment included white gaiters for parades and an IMPERIAL monogram at the lower edge of caps in place of a *keizer-flag*. Also, on the underside of the left brim of officers' hats, above the button, was sewn a small gold tassel, which other regiments did not have (Illus. No. 933) (240).

5 January 1798 - With the changes in organization tables for Grenadier regiments and the addition of the new ranks of *pioneers* (one in each company) and *wagon masters*, these were prescribed the following uniforms and weapons:

Pioneers (fruntovye masterovye)—everything as for privates in their companies, except with the addition of an *apron (zapon ili perednik)* of white (unblackened) leather and an *ax (topor)*. Thus they appeared just like the company carpenters *(rotnye plotniki)* that were part of the Holstein troops of EMPEROR PETER III, already described above (Illus. No. 936) (241).

Wagon master (vagenmeister)—everything as for Fusilier non-commissioned officers except for halberds and hats, the latter for a wagon master being the three-cornered officers' pattern *hat* described above, with a black draw cord and a button the same color as on the coat. The hat's brim was trimmed with gold or silver galloon (according to the color of the buttons), 1/3 vershok (3/5 inch) wide, sewn on so that it is almost all visible. On all three corners is a white woolen tassel, mixed with black and orange (Illus. No. 936) (242).

Along with this, there were the following changes in uniform clothing, weapons, and accouterments for Grenadier regiments:

1) Tassels on grenadier caps were ordered to be: white for privates in the 1st Battalion, red for privates in the 2nd Battalion, and for non-commissioned officers—white with black and orange (243).

2) Instead of white greatcoats, similarly white cloth *cloaks (plashchi)* were issued, of the exact same pattern as used during the last years of EMPRESS CATHERINE II's reign. It was also left to the Regimental *Chefs* as to whether these were to be made with or without hoods *(kapishony)* (244).

3) On sword belts and cross belts the side stitching *(proshivki)* was abolished, and instead it was ordered to put, after whitening, grooves or gutters *(zhelobki ili dorozhki)* near the edges (245).

4) The frames or hoops of drums were ordered to be painted in dark-green and white (246).

5) Halberd and spontoon shafts and drumsticks were ordered to be painted the same color as the regiment's flag poles (247), and consequently they were of the following colors:

In the Yekaterinoslav Regiment — straw-colored.
— Astrakhan — white.
— Little-Russia — black.
— Kiev   — white.
— Siberia — white.
— Phanagoria   — white.
— Kherson — black.
— Caucasus — white.
— Moscow — straw-colored.
— Taurica — straw-colored.
— Pavlovsk — straw-colored .
— Leib-Grenadier — straw-colored (248).

31 January 1799 - The cloaks established by the warrant of 5 January 1798 were replaced by *greatcoats* of dark-green cloth, without buttons (249).

9 October 1799 - The knots *(shishki)* on officers' sashes and sword knots, on hat tassels, and also on lower ranks' sword knots, are ordered to be raspberry-colored *(malinovyi)*, and stripes and tassels are to have three colors: black, orange, and raspberry (250).

25 January 1801 - Regimental generals and field and company-grade officers, who were prescribed spurs, were ordered to have these in the same color as their buttons (251).

II. MUSKETEER REGIMENTS *(Mushketerskie polki)*

29 November 1796 - The changes that took place in the clothing and weapons of Grenadier regiments were extended with equal force to Musketeer regiments, namely:

Private musketeers (ryadovye mushketery)—everything prescribed the same as for fusiliers except for the caps being replaced by the hats already described above, on which trim was of white woolen tape. The upper part of the tassel was of the two regimental colors, i.e. those on the coat, collar, lapels, cuffs, and shoulder strap, and the side tassels with the cord connecting them were yellow with black. At first white bows were prescribed for the hats, but soon they were removed (252).

Musketeer non-commissioned officers—the same as for Fusilier non-commissioned officers, but again with the cap replaced by a hat which was trimmed with gold or silver galloon in accordance with the buttons, and which had woolen tassels: on the sides—yellow with black, and at the top—of both regimental colors (253).

Musketeer drummers—the same as for Fusilier drummers, with the cap changed for the musketeer hat described above (254).

Grenadiers, non-commissioned officers, drummers, and *fifers*—the same as the corresponding ranks in Grenadier or Wing companies of Grenadier regiments (255).

Regimental drummer and *musicians*—the same as in Grenadier regiments, but with non-commissioned officers' hats instead of caps (256).

Officers, generals, and all *noncombatants*—as for these ranks in Grenadier regiments, without any changes (257).

Distinctions in colors and various parts of the uniform for Musketeer regiments were as follows:

In the Belozersk Regiment:
Lower ranks—coat with straw-colored collar, lapels, cuffs, and shoulder strap; white buttonhole loops on the sleeves, without small tassels; white waistcoat and breeches; white buttons (Illus. No. 937); straw-colored back piece on the grenadier cap; trim—yellow with black; and dark-green band; halberd shafts and drumsticks black; drum hoops dark green with straw. *Officers*—silver buttonhole loops, without small tassels; black spontoon shafts (258).

In the Nasheburg Regiment: Lower ranks—coat with grey *(seryi)* collar, lapels, cuffs, and shoulder strap; white buttonhole loops on the sleeves, with small tassels; white waistcoat and breeches; yellow buttons; grey back piece on the grenadier cap; trim—yellow with black; and dark-green band; halberd shafts and drumsticks black; drum hoops dark green with grey (Illus. No. 938). *Officers*—silver buttonhole loops, with small tassels without metallic thread; black spontoon shafts (259).

In the Chernigov Regiment:
Lower ranks—coat without collar or lapels, rose *(rozovye)* cuffs and shoulder strap; orange *(pomerantsovye)* buttonhole loops on the sleeves, without small tassels; white waistcoat and breeches; yellow buttons (Illus. No. 939); rose back piece on the grenadier cap; trim—yellow with black; and dark-green band; halberd shafts and drumsticks black; drum hoops dark green with rose. *Officers*—gold buttonhole loops, without small tassels (Illus. No. 939); black spontoon shafts (260).

In the New-Ingermanland Regiment:
Lower ranks—coat without lapels, scarlet collar, cuffs and shoulder strap; orange buttonhole loops on the sleeves, with black checkered tracing; white waistcoat and breeches; yellow buttons; dark-scarlet back piece on the grenadier cap; trim—yellow with black; and dark-green band (Illus. No. 940); halberd shafts and drumsticks black; drum hoops dark green with scarlet. *Officers*—gold buttonhole loops, with black silk, of the same pattern as for lower ranks (Illus. No. 940); black spontoon shafts (261).

In the Yaroslavl Regiment: Lower ranks—coat without lapels, raspberry collar, cuffs and shoulder strap; white buttonhole loops on the sleeves; white waistcoat and breeches; white buttons; raspberry back piece on the grenadier cap; trim—yellow with black; and dark-green band (Illus. No. 941); halberd shafts and drumsticks black; drum hoops dark green with raspberry. *Officers*-silver buttonhole loops (Illus. No. 941); black spontoon shafts (262).

In the Apsheron Regiment: Lower ranks—coat without collar or lapels, red cuffs and shoulder strap; white buttonhole loops on the sleeves, without small tassels; white waistcoat and breeches; yellow buttons; red back piece on the grenadier cap; trim—yellow with black; and dark-green band; halberd shafts and drumsticks straw-colored; drum hoops dark green with red (Illus. No. 942). *Officers*—gold buttonhole loops without small tassels; straw-colored spontoon shafts (263).

In the Smolensk Regiment: Lower ranks—coat with puce (*pyusovyi*) collar, lapels, cuffs, and shoulder strap; white buttonhole loops; straw-colored waistcoat and breeches; white buttons; puce back piece on the grenadier cap; trim—yellow with black; and dark-green band (Illus. No. 943); halberd shafts and drumsticks black; drum hoops dark green with puce. *Officers*—silver buttonhole loops; black spontoon shafts (264).

In the Ryazhsk Regiment: Lower ranks—coat with apple-green (*verdepompovyi*, i.e. "*vert de pomme*") collar, lapels, cuffs, and shoulder strap; yellow buttonhole loops on the sleeves, with small tassels; white waistcoat and breeches; yellow buttons (Illus. No. 944); apple-green back piece on the grenadier cap; trim—yellow with black; and dark-green band; halberd shafts and drumsticks black; drum hoops dark green with apple-green. *Officers*—gold buttonhole loops with small tassels, without metallic thread (Illus. No. 944); black spontoon shafts (265).

In the Kursk Regiment: Lower ranks—coat with white collar, lapels, cuffs, and shoulder strap; white buttonhole loops on the sleeves, without small tassels; white waistcoat and breeches; white buttons; white back piece on the grenadier cap; trim—yellow with black; and dark-green band (Illus. No. 945); halberd shafts and drumsticks black; drum hoops dark green with white. *Officers*—silver buttonhole loops without small tassels, with flattened wire thread; black spontoon shafts (266).

In the Kozlov Regiment: Lower ranks—coat with rose collar, lapels, cuffs, and shoulder strap; white buttonhole loops on the sleeves, with small tassels; white waistcoat and breeches; white buttons; rose back piece on the grenadier cap; trim—yellow with black; and dark-green band (Illus. No. 946); halberd shafts and drumsticks black; drum hoops dark green with rose. *Officers*—silver buttonhole loops, embroidered, with small tassels; black spontoon shafts (267).

In the Sevastopol Regiment: Lower ranks—coat with sand-colored (*pesochnyi*) collar, cuffs, lapels, and shoulder strap; white buttonhole loops on the sleeves, with sky-blue tracery and small tassels; white waistcoat and breeches; yellow buttons (Illus. No. 947); sand-colored back piece on the grenadier cap; trim—yellow with black; and dark-green band; halberd shafts and drumsticks straw-colored; drum hoops dark green with sand. *Officers*—gold buttonhole loops, with small tassels (Illus. No. 947); straw-colored spontoon shafts (268).

In the Belevsk Regiment:

Lower ranks—coat with collar, cuffs, lapels, and shoulder strap entirely dark green; yellow buttonhole loops on the sleeves, with red circles (*kruzhkami*) and with small tassels; white waistcoat and breeches; white buttons; dark-green back piece and band on the grenadier cap, and trim— yellow with black (Illus. No. 948); halberd shafts and drumsticks black; drum hoops dark green. *Officers*—silver buttonhole loops, with small tassels; black spontoon shafts (269).

In the Aleksopol Regiment: Lower ranks—coat without lapels, with camel-colored (*verblyuzhii*) collar, cuffs, and shoulder strap; white buttonhole loops on the sleeves, with small tassels; white waistcoat and breeches; white buttons; camel-colored back piece on the grenadier cap; trim— yellow with black; and dark-green band (Illus. No. 949); halberd shafts and drumsticks black; drum hoops dark green with camel. *Officers*—silver buttonhole loops, with small tassels; black spontoon shafts (270).

In the Schlüsselburg Regiment: Lower ranks—coat with apple-green collar, cuffs, lapels, and shoulder strap; white buttonhole loops on the sleeves, without small tassels; white waistcoat and breeches; white buttons; apple-green back piece on the grenadier cap; trim—yellow with black; and dark-green band (Illus. No. 950); halberd shafts and drumsticks black; drum hoops dark green with apple green. *Officers*—silver buttonhole loops, with metallic thread, without small tassels; black spontoon shafts (271).

In the Bryansk Regiment:

Lower ranks—coat without lapels, orange (*oranzhevyi*) collar, cuffs, and shoulder strap; yellow buttonhole loops on the sleeves, without small tassels; white waistcoat and breeches; yellow buttons (Illus. No. 951); orange back piece on the grenadier cap; trim—yellow with black; and dark-green band; halberd shafts and drumsticks black; drum hoops dark green with orange. *Officers*—gold buttonhole loops, without small tassels, with metallic thread; black spontoon shafts (272).

In the Troitsk Regiment:

Lower ranks—coat with light-violet (*svetlo-fioletovyi*) collar, cuffs, lapels, and shoulder strap; straw-colored buttonhole loops on the sleeves, with yellow stripes and circles, without small tassels; white waistcoat and breeches; yellow buttons (Illus. No. 952); light-violet back piece on the grenadier cap; trim—yellow with black; and dark-green band; halberd shafts and drumsticks black; drum hoops dark green with light violet. *Officers*—gold buttonhole loops, with metallic thread, without small tassels; black spontoon shafts (273).

In the Ladoga Regiment:

Lower ranks—coat with brown (*korichnevyi*) collar, cuffs, lapels, and shoulder strap; white buttonhole loops on the sleeves, with brown edges and small yellow tassels; white waistcoat and breeches; yellow buttons; brown back piece on the grenadier cap; trim—yellow with black; and dark-green band (Illus. No. 953); halberd shafts and drumsticks black; drum hoops dark green with brown. *Officers*—silver buttonhole loops, with brown silk edges and small gold tassels; black spontoon shafts (274).

In the Polotsk Regiment: Lower ranks—coat with light-green collar, cuffs, lapels, and shoulder strap; white buttonhole loops on the sleeves, without small tassels; white waistcoat and breeches;

white buttons; light-green back piece on the grenadier cap; trim—yellow with black; and dark-green band (Illus. No. 954); halberd shafts and drumsticks black; drum hoops dark green with light green. *Officers*—silver buttonhole loops, with metallic thread, without small tassels; black spontoon shafts (275).

In the Archangel Regiment: Lower ranks—coat with grey (*seryi*) collar, lapels, cuffs, and shoulder strap; white buttonhole loops on the sleeves, with black tracery, without small tassels; straw-colored waistcoat and breeches; white buttons (Illus. No. 955); grey back piece on the grenadier cap; trim—yellow with black; and dark-green band; halberd shafts and drumsticks black; drum hoops dark green with grey. *Officers*—silver buttonhole loops, without small tassels; black spontoon shafts (276).

In the Old-Ingermanland Regiment: Lower ranks—coat with camel-colored collar, lapels, cuffs, and shoulder strap; yellow buttonhole loops on the sleeves, without small tassels; white waistcoat and breeches; yellow buttons; camel-colored back piece on the grenadier cap; trim—yellow with black; and dark-green band (Illus. No. 956); halberd shafts and drumsticks straw-colored; drum hoops dark green with camel. *Officers*—gold buttonhole loops, with a stripe down the center made from metallic thread, without small tassels (Illus. No. 956); straw-colored spontoon shafts (277).

In the Novgorod Regiment: Lower ranks—coat with apricot (*abrikosvyi*) collar, lapels, cuffs, and shoulder strap; yellow buttonhole loops on the sleeves, without small tassels; white waistcoat and breeches; yellow buttons; apricot back piece on the grenadier cap; trim—yellow with black; and dark-green band; halberd shafts and drumsticks black; drum hoops dark green with apricot (Illus. No. 957). *Officers*—gold buttonhole loops, with two stripes made from metallic thread, without small tassels; black spontoon shafts (278).

In the Nizhnii-Novgorod Regiment:
Lower ranks—coat with rose collar, lapels, cuffs, and shoulder strap; white buttonhole loops on the sleeves; (waistcoat, breeches, and button information not provided - M.C.); rose back piece on the grenadier cap; trim—yellow with black; and dark-green band (Illus. No. 958); halberd shafts and drumsticks black; drum hoops dark green with rose. *Officers*—silver buttonhole loops, with metallic thread, without small tassels; black spontoon shafts (279).

In the Vitebsk Regiment:
Lower ranks—coat with pale-rose (*bledno-rozovyi*) collar, lapels, cuffs, and shoulder strap; yellow buttonhole loops on the sleeves, with small tassels; straw-colored waistcoat and breeches; yellow buttons (Illus. No. 959); pale-rose back piece on the grenadier cap; trim—yellow with black; and dark-green band; halberd shafts and drumsticks straw-colored; drum hoops dark green with pale rose. *Officers*—gold buttonhole loops, with small tassels; straw-colored spontoon shafts (280).

In the Azov Regiment:
Lower ranks—coat with white collar, lapels, cuffs, and shoulder strap; yellow buttonhole loops on the sleeves, without small tassels; white waistcoat and breeches; white buttons (Illus. No. 960); white back piece on the grenadier cap; trim—yellow with black; and dark-green band; halberd shafts and drumsticks black; drum hoops dark green with white. *Officers*—gold buttonhole loops, without small tassels; black spontoon shafts (281).

In the Orel Regiment:
Lower ranks—coat with white collar, lapels, cuffs, and shoulder strap; white buttonhole loops on

the sleeves, with green stripes and with small tassels; straw-colored waistcoat and breeches; white buttons; white back piece on the grenadier cap; trim—yellow with black; and dark-green band (Illus. No. 960); halberd shafts and drumsticks black; drum hoops dark green with white. *Officers*—silver buttonhole loops, with small tassels and green stripes along the edges; black spontoon shafts (282).

In the Reval Regiment:
Lower ranks—coat with cherry (*vishnevyi*) collar, lapels, cuffs, and shoulder strap; white buttonhole loops on the sleeves, with small tassels; straw-colored waistcoat and breeches; white buttons (Illus. No. 961); cherry back piece on the grenadier cap; trim—yellow with black; and dark-green band; halberd shafts and drumsticks black; drum hoops dark green with cherry. *Officers*—silver buttonhole loops, without metallic thread, with small tassels (Illus. No. 961); black spontoon shafts (283).

In the Tula Regiment:
Lower ranks—coat without lapels, red collar, slit cuffs, and shoulder strap; yellow buttonhole loops on the sleeves, without small tassels; straw-colored waistcoat and breeches; yellow buttons; red back piece on the grenadier cap; trim—yellow with black; and dark-green band (Illus. No. 962); halberd shafts and drumsticks black; drum hoops dark green with red. *Officers*—gold buttonhole loops, without metallic thread and without small tassels; black spontoon shafts (284).

In the Yelets Regiment:
Lower ranks—coat with raspberry (*malinovyi*) collar, lapels, cuffs, and shoulder strap; yellow buttonhole loops on the sleeves with two wide green stripes, without small tassels; white waistcoat and breeches; yellow buttons (Illus. No. 963); plate on the grenadier cap with a HIGHEST monogram at the bottom, raspberry back piece on the grenadier cap; trim—yellow with black; and green band; halberd shafts and drumsticks black; drum hoops dark green with raspberry. *Officers*-gold buttonhole loops, with two wide green stripes, without small tassels; black spontoon shafts (285).

In the Pskov Regiment:
Lower ranks—coat with apple-green collar, lapels, cuffs, and shoulder strap; yellow buttonhole loops on the sleeves, without small tassels; white waistcoat and breeches; yellow buttons; apple-green back piece on the grenadier cap; trim—yellow with black; and dark-green band (Illus. No. 964); halberd shafts and drumsticks black; drum hoops dark green with apple green. *Officers*—gold buttonhole loops, without metallic thread and without small tassels; black spontoon shafts (286).

In the Tambov Regiment:
Lower ranks—coat with celadon-green (*seladonovyi*, a greenish yellow or sea green) collar, lapels, cuffs, and shoulder strap; white buttonhole loops on the sleeves, without small tassels; white waistcoat and breeches; yellow buttons; straw-colored back piece on the grenadier cap; trim—yellow with black; and dark-green band (Illus. No. 964); halberd shafts and drumsticks black; drum hoops dark green with celadon green. *Officers*—gold buttonhole loops, without metallic thread and without small tassels; black spontoon shafts (287).

In the Rostov Regiment:
Lower ranks—coat without lapels, red collar, cuffs, and shoulder strap; yellow buttonhole loops on the sleeves, with a red stripe (*struika*) and with small tassels; white waistcoat and breeches; yellow buttons; red back piece on the grenadier cap; trim—yellow with black; and dark-green band (Illus. No. 965); halberd shafts and drumsticks black; drum hoops dark green with red. *Officers*—gold

buttonhole loops, without metallic thread and with a red stripe and small tassels (Illus. No. 965); black spontoon shafts (288).

In the Murom Regiment:

Lower ranks—coat with dark-blue (*temnosinii*) collar, lapels, cuffs, and shoulder strap; white buttonhole loops on the sleeves, without small tassels; white waistcoat and breeches; yellow buttons (Illus. No. 966); dark-blue back piece and band on the grenadier cap; trim—yellow with black; halberd shafts and drumsticks black; drum hoops dark green with dark blue. *Officers*—gold buttonhole loops, without metallic thread or small tassels; black spontoon shafts (289).

In the Staryi-Oskol Regiment:

Lower ranks—coat without collar, lapels, or buttonhole loops, with red slit cuffs and shoulder strap, and in addition to the usual number another button in the slit of the cuffs; white buttonhole loops on the sleeves, without small tassels; white waistcoat and breeches; yellow buttons; white back piece on the grenadier cap; trim—yellow with black, and red band (Illus. No. 967); halberd shafts and drumsticks black; drum hoops dark green with red. *Officers*—coat the same as for lower ranks (Illus. 967); black spontoon shafts (290).

In the Tobolsk Regiment:

Lower ranks—coat with light sky-blue (*svetlo-goluboi*) collar, lapels, cuffs, and shoulder strap; white buttonhole loops on the sleeves, with sky-blue tracery and with small tassels; white waistcoat and breeches; white buttons; light sky-blue back piece on the grenadier cap; trim—yellow with black, and dark-green band (Illus. No. 968); halberd shafts and drumsticks black; drum hoops dark green with light sky-blue. *Officers*—silver buttonhole loops, with sky-blue tracery and small tassels; black spontoon shafts (291).

In the Tiflis Regiment:

Lower ranks—coat without lapels, with sand-colored collar, cuffs, and shoulder strap; white buttonhole loops on the sleeves, without small tassels; straw-colored waistcoat and breeches; sand-colored back piece on the grenadier cap; trim—yellow with black, and dark-green band (Illus. No. 969); halberd shafts and drumsticks black; drum hoops dark green with sand. *Officers*—silver buttonhole loops, with metallic thread, without tassels; black spontoon shafts (292).

In the Voronezh Regiment:

Lower ranks—coat with straw-colored collar, lapels, cuffs, and shoulder strap; yellow buttonhole loops on the sleeves, without small tassels; white waistcoat and breeches; yellow buttons (Illus. No. 970); straw-colored back piece on the grenadier cap; trim—yellow with black, and dark-green band; halberd shafts and drumsticks black; drum hoops dark green with straw. *Officers*—gold buttonhole loops, with metallic thread, and without small tassels; black spontoon shafts (293).

In the Kazan Regiment: Lower ranks—coat without collar or lapels, with yellow cuffs and shoulder strap; yellow buttonhole loops on the sleeves, without small tassels; white waistcoat and breeches; yellow buttons (Illus. No. 971); yellow back piece on the grenadier cap; trim—yellow with black, and dark-green band; halberd shafts and drumsticks black; drum hoops dark green with yellow. *Officers*—gold buttonhole loops, with metallic thread, and without small tassels (Illus. No. 971); black spontoon shafts (294).

In the Moscow Regiment: Lower ranks—coat with dark-blue (*temno-sinii*) collar, lapels, cuffs, and shoulder strap; yellow buttonhole loops on the sleeves, with small tassels; straw-colored waistcoat and breeches; yellow buttons; dark-blue back piece on the grenadier cap; trim—yellow with black, and dark-green band (Illus. No. 972); halberd shafts and drumsticks black; drum hoops dark green with dark blue. *Officers*—gold buttonhole loops, with small tassels; black spontoon shafts (295).

In the Kabarda Regiment: Lower ranks—coat without collar or lapels, with red cuffs and shoulder strap; yellow buttonhole loops on the sleeves, with small white tassels; white waistcoat and breeches; white buttons; red back piece on the grenadier cap; trim—yellow with black, and dark-green band; halberd shafts and drumsticks straw-colored; drum hoops dark green with red (Illus. No. 973). *Officers*—gold buttonhole loops, with small silver tassels (Illus. No. 973); straw-colored spontoon shafts (296).

In the Vladimir Regiment:

Lower ranks—coat with red collar, lapels, slit cuffs, and shoulder strap; yellow buttonhole loops on the cuffs, with red edges and without small tassels; white waistcoat and breeches; yellow buttons; black neck cloth (Illus. No. 974); red back piece on the grenadier cap; trim—yellow with black, and dark-green band; halberd shafts and drumsticks black; drum hoops dark green with red. *Officers*—gold buttonhole loops, without small tassels; black neck cloth (Illus. No. 974); black spontoon shafts (297).

In the Uglich Regiment:

Lower ranks—coat with red collar, lapels, cuffs, and shoulder strap; white buttonhole loops on the sleeves, without small tassels; white waistcoat and breeches; white buttons (Illus. No. 975); red back piece on the grenadier cap; trim—yellow with black, and dark-green band; halberd shafts and drumsticks black; drum hoops dark green with red. *Officers*—silver buttonhole loops, without small tassels; black spontoon shafts (298).

In the Sevsk Regiment:

Lower ranks—coat without collar or lapels, with white cuffs and shoulder strap; yellow buttonhole loops on the sleeves, without small tassels; white waistcoat and breeches; yellow buttons (Illus. No. 976); white back piece on the grenadier cap; trim—yellow with black, and dark-green band; halberd shafts and drumsticks black; drum hoops dark green with white. *Officers*—gold buttonhole loops, embroidered, with small tassels; black spontoon shafts (299).

In the Narva Regiment:

Lower ranks—coat without collar, with red lapels, cuffs, and shoulder strap; white buttonhole loops on the sleeves, without small tassels; straw-colored waistcoat and breeches; white buttons (Illus. No. 977); red back piece on the grenadier cap; trim—yellow with black, and dark-green band; halberd shafts and drumsticks black; drum hoops dark green with red. Officers—silver buttonhole loops, without small tassels (Illus. No. 977); black spontoon shafts (300).

In the Dnieper Regiment:

Lower ranks—coat with coffee-colored (*kofeinyi*) collar, lapels, cuffs, and shoulder strap; white buttonhole loops on the sleeves, without small tassels; white waistcoat and breeches; white buttons (Illus. No. 978); coffee-colored back piece on the grenadier cap; trim—yellow with black, and dark-green band; halberd shafts and drumsticks black; drum hoops dark green with coffee. *Officers*—silver buttonhole loops, without small tassels; black spontoon shafts (301).

In the Vyatka Regiment:

Lower ranks—coat without lapels, with sapphire-colored (*yakhontovyi*) collar, cuffs, and shoulder strap; white buttonhole loops on the sleeves, without small tassels; straw-colored waistcoat and breeches; white buttons (Illus. No. 979); sapphire-colored back piece on the grenadier cap; trim—white with black, and dark-green band; halberd shafts and drumsticks black; drum hoops dark green with sapphire. *Officers*—silver buttonhole loops, without small tassels (Illus. No. 979); black spontoon shafts (302).

In the Suzdal Regiment:

Lower ranks—coat without collar or lapels, with red cuffs and shoulder strap; white buttonhole loops on the sleeves, with red edges, without small tassels; white waistcoat and breeches; white buttons (Illus. No. 980); red back piece on the grenadier cap; trim—yellow with black, and dark-green band; halberd shafts and drumsticks black; drum hoops dark green with red. *Officers*—silver buttonhole loops, with red edges, without small tassels (Illus. No. 980); black spontoon shafts (303).

In the Kexholm Regiment:

Lower ranks—coat with rose collar, lapels, cuffs and shoulder strap; yellow buttonhole loops on the sleeves, with small tassels; white waistcoat and breeches; yellow buttons (Illus. No. 981); rose back piece on the grenadier cap; trim—yellow with black, and dark-green band; (halberd and drum information not provided - M.C.). Officers—gold buttonhole loops, without metallic thread, with small tassels; black spontoon shafts (304).

In the Viborg Regiment:

Lower ranks—coat with yellow collar, lapels, cuffs and shoulder strap; yellow buttonhole loops on the sleeves, without small tassels; white waistcoat and breeches; yellow buttons; yellow back piece on the grenadier cap; trim—yellow with black, and dark-green band; halberd shafts and drumsticks black; drum hoops dark green with yellow (Illus. No. 982). Officers-gold buttonhole loops, without metallic thread or small tassels; black spontoon shafts (305).

In the Ryazan Regiment:

Lower ranks—coat with light-raspberry collar, lapels, cuffs and shoulder strap; white buttonhole loops on the sleeves, with small tassels next to the buttons; white waistcoat and breeches; white buttons; light-raspberry back piece on the grenadier cap; trim—white with black, and dark-green band (Illus. No. 983); halberd shafts and drumsticks straw-colored; drum hoops dark green with light raspberry. *Officers*—silver buttonhole loops, with small tassels next to the buttons; straw-colored spontoon shafts (306).

In the Neva Regiment:

Lower ranks—coat without collar, with red lapels, cuffs and shoulder strap; yellow buttonhole loops on the sleeves, with small tassels; white waistcoat and breeches; yellow buttons; red back piece on the grenadier cap; trim—yellow, and dark-green band (Illus. No. 984); halberd shafts and drumsticks black; drum hoops dark green with red. *Officers*—gold buttonhole loops, with small tassels of twisted fringe (*iz vitoi kaniteli*); black spontoon shafts (307).

In the Velikie-Luki Regiment:

Lower ranks—coat with red collar, lapels, cuffs and shoulder strap; yellow buttonhole loops on the sleeves, with small tassels; white waistcoat and breeches; yellow buttons (Illus. No. 984); red back piece on the grenadier cap; trim—yellow with black, and dark-green band; halberd shafts and drumsticks straw-colored; drum hoops dark green with red. *Officers*—gold buttonhole loops, with small tassels of twisted fringe; straw-colored spontoon shafts (308).

In the Sofiya Regiment:
Lower ranks—coat with red collar, lapels, cuffs and shoulder strap; red buttonhole loops on the sleeves, with yellow and black tracery, without small tassels; white waistcoat and breeches; yellow buttons; red back piece on the grenadier cap; trim—yellow with black, band—dark-green with red (Illus. No. 985); (halberd and drum information not provided - M.C.). *Officers*—embroidered buttonholes, gold and black silk on red silk, without small tassels (Illus. No. 985); black spontoon shafts (309).

In the Shirvan Regiment:
Lower ranks—coat without lapels, with straw-colored collar, cuffs and shoulder strap; white buttonhole loops on the sleeves, with small tassels; straw-colored waistcoat and breeches; white buttons (Illus. No. 986); straw-colored back piece on the grenadier cap; trim—yellow with black, and dark-green band; halberd shafts and drumsticks straw-colored; drum hoops dark green with straw. *Officers*—silver buttonhole loops, with small tassel (Illus. No. 986); straw-colored spontoon shafts (310).

In the Perm Regiment:
Lower ranks—coat with sapphire (*yakhontovyi*) collar, lapels, cuffs and shoulder strap; yellow buttonhole loops on the sleeves, with small tassels; white waistcoat and breeches; yellow buttons; sapphire back piece on the grenadier cap; trim—yellow, and dark-green band (Illus. No. 987); halberd shafts and drumsticks black; drum hoops dark green with sapphire. *Officers*—gold buttonhole loops, without metallic thread, with small tassels; black spontoon shafts (311).

In the Nizovsk Regiment:
Lower ranks—coat without collar, with red lapels, cuffs and shoulder strap; buttonhole loops on the sleeves yellow with two black stripes, without small tassels; white waistcoat and breeches; yellow buttons (Illus. No. 988); red back piece on the grenadier cap; trim—yellow with black, and dark-green band; halberd shafts and drumsticks black; drum hoops dark green with red. *Officers*—buttonhole loops gold with two stripes, without metallic thread or small tassels (Illus. No. 988); black spontoon shafts (312).

In the Butyrsk Regiment:
Lower ranks—coat with plank-colored (*planshevyi*, from French *planche*) collar, lapels, cuffs and shoulder strap; white buttonhole loops on the sleeves, without small tassels; white waistcoat and breeches; yellow buttons; plank-colored back piece on the grenadier cap; trim—yellow with black, and dark-green band; halberd shafts and drumsticks black; drum hoops dark green with plank. *Officers*—silver buttonhole loops, with metallic thread, without small tassels (Illus. No. 989); black spontoon shafts (313).

In the Ufa Regiment:
Lower ranks—coat with grey (*dikii*) collar, lapels, cuffs and shoulder strap; white buttonhole loops on the sleeves, with small tassels; white waistcoat and breeches; white buttons; grey back piece on the grenadier cap; trim—yellow with black, and dark-green band (Illus. No. 990); halberd shafts and drumsticks straw-colored; drum hoops dark green with grey. *Officers*—silver buttonhole loops, with small tassels; straw-colored spontoon shafts (314).

In the Rylsk Regiment:
Lower ranks—coat with fire-colored (bright, orange) (*ognevyi* (*yarkii, oranzhevyi*)) collar, lapels,

cuffs and shoulder strap; white checkered buttonhole loops on the sleeves, without small tassels; white waistcoat and breeches; white buttons (Illus. No. 991); fire-colored back piece on the grenadier cap; trim—yellow with black, and dark-green band (Illus. No. 991); halberd shafts and drumsticks straw-colored; drum hoops dark green with fire. *Officers*—silver buttonhole loops, checkered, of metallic thread, without small tassels (Illus. No. 991); straw-colored spontoon shafts (315).

In the Yekaterinburg Regiment:

Lower ranks—coat without lapels, with puce collar, cuffs and shoulder strap; yellow buttonhole loops on the sleeves, with small tassels; white waistcoat and breeches; yellow buttons (Illus. No. 992); puce back piece on the grenadier cap; trim—yellow with black, and dark-green band; halberd shafts and drumsticks black; drum hoops dark green with puce. *Officers*—gold buttonhole loops, with small tassels (Illus. No. 992); black spontoon shafts (316).

In the Selenginsk Regiment:

Lower ranks—coat without collar, with grey (*dikii*) lapels, cuffs and shoulder strap; yellow buttonhole loops on the sleeves, without small tassels; straw-colored waistcoat and breeches; yellow buttons; grey back piece on the grenadier cap; trim—yellow with black, and dark-green band (Illus. No. 993); halberd shafts and drumsticks black; drum hoops dark green with grey. *Officers*—gold buttonhole loops, with metallic thread, without small tassels; black spontoon shafts (317).

In the Tomsk Regiment:

Lower ranks—coat without lapels, with raspberry collar, cuffs and shoulder strap; yellow buttonhole loops on the sleeves, with black tracery and with small tassels; straw-colored waistcoat and breeches; white buttons (Illus. No. 994); raspberry back piece on the grenadier cap; trim—yellow with black, and dark-green band; halberd shafts and drumsticks straw-colored; drum hoops dark green with raspberry. *Officers*—buttonhole loops gold with black silk, with small tassels (Illus. No. 994); straw-colored spontoon shafts (318).

In Arkharov's Regiment:

Lower ranks—coat with light-rose collar, lapels, cuffs and shoulder strap; white buttonhole loops on the sleeves, without small tassels; white waistcoat and breeches; (No button information provided - M.C.); plates with a black eagle on grenadier caps; light-rose back piece and band; trim—white with black (Illus. No. 995); halberd shafts and drumsticks black; drum hoops dark green with light rose. *Officers*—silver buttonhole loops, without metallic thread or small tassels; black spontoon shafts (319).

5 January 1798 - With the change in organization tables for Musketeer regiments and the introduction of *pioneers and wagon masters* in them as for Grenadier regiments, these ranks are given the same uniforms as for Grenadiers, except that pioneers in Musketeer companies have a hat instead of a grenadier cap, of the same pattern as for privates' *hats* (Illus. 996) (320). Along with this, as similarly related above for Grenadier regiments, there were several general changes in Musketeer regiments, namely:

1) Tassels on grenadier caps were ordered to be: white for privates in the 1st Battalion, red for privates in the 2nd Battalion, and for non-commissioned officers-white with black and orange (321).

2) White greatcoats were replaced by similarly white *cloaks*, with or without hoods (322).

3) On sword belts and cross belts the side stitching (*proshivki*) was abolished, and instead it was ordered to have grooves or gutters (*zhelobki ili dorozhki*) (323).

4) The outside of drum hoops was ordered to be painted in only two colors: dark-green and white (324).
5) Halberd and spontoon shafts and drumsticks were ordered to be painted the same color as the regiment's flag poles (325), and consequently they were:

— Belozersk Regiment — black.
— Nasheburg — coffee.
— Chernigov — black.
— New-Ingermanland — coffee.
— Yaroslavl — straw-colored.
— Apsheron — black.
— Smolensk — straw-colored.
— Ryazhsk — black.
— Kursk — black.
— Kozlov — white.
— Sevastopol — black.
— Belevsk — coffee.
— Aleksopol — black.
— Schlüsselburg — black.
— Bryansk — coffee.
— Troitsk — straw-colored.
— Ladoga — black.
— Polotsk — black.
— Archangel — black.
— Old-Ingermanland — white.
— Novgorod — white.
— Nizhnii-Novgorod — coffee.
— Vitebsk — white.
— Azov — straw-colored.
— Orel — straw-colored.
— Reval — white.
— Tula — coffee.
— Yelets — black.
— Pskov — straw-colored.
— Tambov — black.
— Rostov — coffee.
— Murom — coffee.
— Staryi-Oskol — white.
— Tobolsk — white.
— Tiflis — black.
— Voronezh — white.
— Kazan — straw-colored.
— Moscow — white.

— Kabarda — white.
— Vladimir — white.
— Uglich — straw-colored.
— Sevsk — black.
— Narva — white.
— Dnieper — straw-colored.
— Vyatka — coffee.
— Suzdal — straw-colored.
— Kexholm — coffee.
— Viborg — coffee.
— Ryazan — white.
— Neva — black.
— Velikie-Luki — black.
— Sofiya — coffee.
— Shirvan — white.
— Perm — white.
— Nizovsk — white.
— Butyrsk — black.
— Ufa — black.
— Rylsk — coffee.
— Yekaterinburg — coffee.
— Selenginsk — black.
— Tomsk — coffee.
— Arkharov's — coffee (316).

In the Musketeer regiments of *Pavlutskii, Leitner, Brant, Müller 1st, Marklovskii 1st*, and *Berg*, established on 20 August 1798, the uniforms and distinctive colors, based on the Military Regulation of 29 November 1796 and an organization table of 5 January 1798, were as follows:
In Pavlutskii's Regiment:
Lower ranks—coat without lapels, with orange (*oranzhevyi*) collar, cuffs and shoulder strap; yellow buttonhole loops on the sleeves, without small tassels; yellow waistcoat and breeches; yellow buttons; white back piece and band on the grenadier cap; trim—white with black (Illus. No. 996); halberd shafts and drumsticks straw-colored; drum hoops dark green with white. *Officers*—gold buttonhole loops, without small tassels; straw-colored spontoon shafts (327).
In Leitner's Regiment: Lower ranks—coat without lapels, with orange (*oranzhevyi*) collar, cuffs and shoulder strap; white buttonhole loops on the sleeves, without small tassels; yellow waistcoat and breeches; white buttons; white back piece and band on the grenadier cap; trim—white with black (Illus. No. 997); halberd shafts and drumsticks white; drum hoops dark green with white. *Officers*—silver buttonhole loops, without small tassels; white spontoon shafts (328).
In Brant's Regiment: Lower ranks—coat without lapels, with light-green collar, cuffs and shoulder strap; buttonhole loops on the sleeves-white with light-green stripes, without small tassels; white waistcoat and breeches; yellow buttons; straw-colored back piece and band on the grenadier cap,

white trim (Illus. No. 998); halberd shafts and drumsticks white; drum hoops dark green with white. *Officers*—gold buttonhole loops, without small tassels; white spontoon shafts (329).

In Müller 1st's Regiment: Lower ranks—coat without lapels, with apple-green collar, cuffs and shoulder strap; white buttonhole loops on the sleeves, with light-green tracery, without small tassels; white waistcoat and breeches; white buttons; yellow back piece and band on the grenadier cap, white trim (Illus. No. 999); halberd shafts and drumsticks white; drum hoops dark green with white. *Officers*—silver buttonhole loops, without small tassels; white spontoon shafts (330).

In Marklovskii 1st's Regiment: Lower ranks—coat without lapels, with white collar, cuffs and shoulder strap; white buttonhole loops on the sleeves, with small tassels; yellow waistcoat and breeches; yellow buttons; sky-blue back piece and band on the grenadier cap, trim—white with black (Illus. No. 1000); halberd shafts and drumsticks white; drum hoops dark green with white. *Officers*—gold buttonhole loops, with small tassels; white spontoon shafts (331).

In Berg's Regiment: Lower ranks—coat without lapels, with white collar, cuffs and shoulder strap; white buttonhole loops on the sleeves, without small tassels; yellow waistcoat and breeches; white buttons; sky-blue back piece and band on the grenadier cap, white trim; halberd shafts and drumsticks white; drum hoops dark green with white (Illus. No. 1001). *Officers*—silver buttonhole loops, without small tassels; white spontoon shafts (332).

31 January 1799 - The cloaks established by the warrant of 5 January 1798 are replaced by *greatcoats* of the pattern described above for grenadiers (333).

9 October 1799 - The knots (*shishki*) on officers' sashes and sword knots, on hat tassels, and also on lower ranks' sword knots, are ordered to be raspberry-colored, and stripes and tassels are to have three colors: black, orange, and raspberry (334).

14 June 1800 - Maj.-Gen. Ushakov 1st's Musketeer Regiment, renamed from the Senate Regiment, is prescribed the following uniform and distinctive colors: *lower ranks*—dark-green coat without lapels, with red collar, cuffs, shoulder strap, and lining; aiguillette of white silk with silver; white buttonhole loops on the cuffs for all combatant lower ranks, white sewn-on stripes for drummers and fifers, of fine quality canvas tape (*iz kanifasnoi tes'my*); sewn-on silver galloon for musicians; yellow waistcoat and breeches for all; white buttons; black neck cloth, with white leather edging; hats with white trim (Illus. No. 1002) silvered plates on grenadier caps; red back piece; silver trim, yellow band (Illus. No. 1002); shafts and drumsticks black; drum hoops dark green with white. *Officers*—silver aiguillette and embroidered buttonhole loops, the latter being on the cuffs, pocket flaps, and waist; black neck cloth; hat with general-officer pattern galloon, cockade, and button loop (Illus. No. 1002); black spontoon shafts (335).

(**16 January 1801** — HIS IMPERIAL MAJESTY has noted that in many regiments the galloon on non-commissioned officers' hats is sewn on the outside and inside of the brim contrary to established pattern. It must be sewn almost entirely on the outward side .

25 January 1801 - Regimental generals and field and company-grade officers, who were prescribed spurs, were ordered to have these in the same color as their buttons (336).

III. JÄGER REGIMENTS (*Jägerskie polki*)

Based on the Military Regulation of 29 November 1796, laid out above, and directives attached almost in full to organization tables confirmed by HIGHEST Authority on 5 January 1798, the uniforms, weapons, and accouterments of *Jäger battalions*, soon named *regiments*, were as follows: *Jäger privates*—coat (*kaftan*) of light-green (*svetlo-zelenyi*) cloth, without lapels, with folded-down collar, slit cuffs, and buttons (of regimental colors), with a woolen aiguillette the same color as the collar, and with green kersey lining; light-green *waistcoat*, with buttons the same color as on the coat; chamois *breeches* (*chakchiry zamshevyya*) rubbed with chalk, but linen breeches in summer; *boots* with blunt toes, reaching a little higher than the middle of the calf, with a cut-out in back; *neck cloth* of black cloth, without lining, tied in back; musketeer *hat*, without trim; *forage cap* of light-green cloth, with a band the same color as the collar; *greatcoat* of dark-green cloth, with covered buttons, *warm coat* (*fufaika ili polushubok*); *rifle* (*shtutser*) with sling, firelock cover, and frizzen cover all of red Russian leather; *hanger* (*kortik*), *sword belt*, and *pouch*—all four the same as used by jägers during the previous reign, and in conclusion, *knapsack*, *water flask*, and *rusk bag*, exactly the same as used in Grenadier and Musketeer regiments (Illus. No. 1003) (337).

Non-commissioned officers—all as for privates, with the addition of *galloon* (the same color as the buttons) on the collar and cuffs; chamois *gloves* with gauntlet cuffs, and canes (Illlus. No. 1004) (338).

Company Waldhornists (*voltornisty*)—the same as privates, with the addition of sewn-on *stripes* on the coat sleeves, of white tape, with a worm (*zmeika*) the same color as the collar, with small tassels at the ends, and without rifle, hanger, or pouch. In place of the last three items, they had a *sword* with a hanger blade (*shpaga s tesachnym klinkom*) of the pattern for grenadiers and musketeers except with a black sword belt and with a *swordknot* whose strap was of black leather and the tassel woolen, in different colors like those in the preceding Army infantry regiments (Illus. No. 1005). Each Waldhornist was prescribed a *Waldhorn* with a woolen plaited cord with tassels, but their details are unknown (339).

Staff-Waldhornists—the same as company Waldhornists, but with *sewn-on tape* along all coat seams and with the addition of: *galloon*, *gloves*, and *cane*, following the style for non-commissioned officers (Illus. No. 1006) (340).

Company-grade officers—coat, waistcoat, *chakchiry breeches*, and *boots*, all exactly the same as for privates except for having gilt or silvered buttons on the first two items, gold or silver aiguillettes according to the color of the buttons; *neck cloth*, of black serge (*sarzha*); *hat* with general-officers' trim (except for the plumage) the same color as the buttons; *gloves* with gauntlet cuffs; *cane*, *sword* (*shpaga*), *sword knot*, *sash*, *gorget*, and *spontoon*; all, beginning with the neck cloth, of the patterns for officers in the rest of the infantry, and the last item with a black shaft (Illus. No. 1007) (341).

Adjutants—all as for other company-grade officers but with high bell-top boots with spurs and gaiter cuffs (Illus. 1008); shabracks and pistol holders of light-green cloth with one row of galloon the same color as the buttons (342).

Field-grade officers—the same as adjutants (343).

Generals—the same as field-grade officers except with white plumage on the hat (Illus. No. 1009) (344).

Like grenadiers and musketeers, *jäger officers and generals* were prescribed *frock coats* and *greatcoats (sertuki i shineli)* (345).

Colors for collars, cuffs, and buttons in Jäger regiments were as follows (346):
In the 1st — straw-colored collar and cuff; yellow buttons (Illus. No. 1003).
In the 2nd— red collar and cuff; yellow buttons (Illus. No. 1004).
In the 3rd — puce collar and cuffs; white buttons (Illus. No. 1005).
In the 4th — fire-colored (*ognevyi*) collar and cuffs; yellow buttons (Illus. No. 1006).
In the 5th — violet collar and cuffs; yellow buttons (Illus. No. 1007).
In the 6th — orange (*oranzhevyi*) collar and cuffs; yellow buttons (Illus. No. 1008).
In the 7th — brick-red (*krasno-kirpichnyi*) collar and cuffs; yellow buttons (Illus. No. 1009).
In the 8th — white collar and cuffs; yellow buttons (Illus. No. 1010).
In the 9th — coffee-colored (*kofeinyi*) collar and cuffs; white buttons (Illus. No. 1011).
In the 10th — brown collar and cuffs; white buttons (Illus. No. 1011).
In the 11th — plank-colored (*planshevyi*) collar and cuffs; yellow buttons (Illus. No. 1012).
In the 12th — coffee-colored collar and cuffs; white buttons (Illus. No. 1012).
In the 13th — light-green collar and cuffs; yellow buttons (Illus. No. 1013).
In the 14th — rose collar and cuffs; yellow buttons (Illus. No. 1013).
In the 15th — turquoise (*biryuzovyi*) collar and cuffs; white buttons (Illus. No. 1014).
In the 16th — light sky-blue (*svelto-goluboi*) collar and cuffs; white buttons (Illus. No. 1014).
In the 17th — apricot-colored (*abrikosovyi*) collar and cuffs; yellow buttons (Illus. No. 1015).
In the 18th — dark-blue (*sinii*) collar and cuffs; yellow buttons (Illus. No. 1015).
In the 19th — black collar and cuffs; white buttons (Illus. No. 1016).
In the 20th — raspberry collar and cuffs; yellow buttons (Illus. No. 1016).
30 September 1797 - Jäger officers were ordered to no longer have gorgets and spontoons (347).
5 January 1798 - With the introduction of two new ranks in organization tables for Jäger regiments—the *regimental wagon master* and *auditor*—the latter was given the same uniform as for auditors in Grenadier and Musketeer regiments, and the former the same as for Jäger non-commissioned officers except for the rifle, hanger, and pouch, instead of which he was prescribed just a *sword* with a hanger blade (*shpaga s tesachnym klinkom*) and *sword knot* (Illus. No. 1016) (348). Along with this, combatant lower ranks' chamois breeches were replaced by white cloth ones (349).
9 October 1799 - The knots (*shishki*) on officers' sashes and sword knots, on hat tassels, and also on lower ranks' sword knots, were ordered to be raspberry-colored, and stripes and tassels were to have three colors: black, orange, and raspberry (350).
25 January 1801 - Regimental generals and field and company-grade officers, who were prescribed spurs, were ordered to have these in the same color as their buttons (351).

This survey includes all the information available concerning uniform clothing and armament in the Russian field infantry during the reign of EMPEROR PAUL I.

NOTES

(168) Military Regulation of 29 November 1796 and HIGHEST confirmed table of uniforms, accouterments, and weaponry for a Grenadier regiment, 5 January 1798.

(169) Pattern coats preserved by the Commissariat Department of the War Ministry and in HIS IMPERIAL HIGHNESS GRAND DUKE MICHAEL PAVLOVICH's Own Arsenal; Military Regulation of 29 November 1796, Part Ten, Chapter II, Chapter V §§ 2 and 17, and Chapter VI § 9; *Chronicle of the Russian Army*, compiled by Prince Dolgorukov; drawings for this *Chronicle* are located in HIS IMPERIAL MAJESTY'S Own Library under catalog No. 177; HIGHEST confirmed organization table for a Grenadier regiment, 5 January 1798, and evidence from contemporaries.

(170) Pattern waistcoats preserved by the Commissariat Department of the War Ministry. drawings located in HIS IMPERIAL MAJESTY'S Own Library under No. 177; HIGHEST confirmed organization table for a Grenadier regiment, 5 January 1798.

(171) Pattern underclothes preserved by the Commissariat Department of the War Ministry. Military Regulation of 29 November 1796, part ten, Chapter V, addendum to § 6, and Chapter VI, § 6, and HIGHEST confirmed organization table of uniforms, accouterments, and weaponry for a Grenadier regiment, 5 January 1798.

(172) Pattern gaiters preserved by the Commissariat Department of the War Ministry; drawings located in HIS IMPERIAL MAJESTY'S Own Library under No. 177; HIGHEST confirmed table of uniforms, accouterments, and weaponry for a Grenadier regiment, 5 January 1798.

(173) Aforementioned table and evidence from contemporaries.

(174) The same table; drawings located in HIS IMPERIAL MAJESTY'S Own Library under No. 177, and evidence from contemporaries.

(175) Fusilier caps preserved in various Arsenals and at the Commissariat Department of the War Ministry; drawings located in HIS IMPERIAL MAJESTY'S Own Library under No. 177; HIGHEST confirmed table of uniforms, accouterments, and weaponry for a Grenadier regiment, 5 January 1798.

(176) Forage caps preserved in HIS IMPERIAL HIGHNESS GRAND DUKE MICHAEL PAVLOVICH's Own Arsenal; HIGHEST confirmed table of uniforms, accouterments, and weaponry for a Grenadier regiment, 5 January 1798, and evidence from contemporaries.

(177) Pattern greatcoat preserved by the Commissariat Department of the War Ministry.

(178) Military Regulation of 29 November 1796, Part Ten, Chapter VI, § 10, and evidence from contemporaries.

(179) Military Regulation of 29 November 1796, Part Ten, Chapter V, §§ 2 and 12, and HIGHEST confirmed table of uniforms, accouterments, and weaponry for a Grenadier regiment, 5 January 1798.

(180) Military Regulation of 29 November 1796, Part Ten, Chapter VII, §§ 2 and 3; HIGHEST confirmed table of uniforms, accouterments, and weaponry for a Grenadier regiment, 5 January 1798, and evidence from contemporaries.

(181) Military Regulation of 29 November 1796, Part Ten, Chapter VI, note to § 3.

(182) Swords preserved in the St.-Petersburg Arsenal and in HIS IMPERIAL HIGHNESS GRAND DUKE MICHAEL PAVLOVICH's Own Arsenal; HIGHEST confirmed table of uniforms, accouterments, and weaponry for a Grenadier regiment, 5 January 1798.

(183) Military Regulation of 29 November 1796, Part Ten, Chapter VI, note to § 7; pattern sword knots preserved by the Commissariat Department of the War Ministry; drawings located in HIS IMPERIAL MAJESTY'S Own Library under No. 177; HIGHEST confirmed table of uniforms, accouterments, and weaponry for a Grenadier regiment, 5 January 1798, and statements by contemporaries.

(184) Sword belts preserved in HIS IMPERIAL HIGHNESS GRAND DUKE MICHAEL PAVLOVICH's Own Arsenal; drawings located in HIS IMPERIAL MAJESTY'S Own Library under No. 177; Military Regulation of 29 November 1796, Part Ten, Chapter VI, §§ 6 and 9; HIGHEST confirmed table of uniforms, accouterments, and weaponry for a Grenadier regiment, 5 January 1798, and statements by contemporaries.

(185) Bayonet scabbards preserved in the St.-Petersburg Arsenal.

(186) Pattern musket preserved in the St.-Petersburg Arsenal; HIGHEST confirmed table of uniforms, accouterments, and weaponry for a Grenadier regiment, 5 January 1798, and contemporary drawings.

(187) Military Regulation of 29 November 1796, Part Ten, Chapter III, note to § 4.

(188) Pattern frizzen cover preserved by the Commissariat Department of the War Ministry, and HIGHEST confirmed table of uniforms, accouterments, and weaponry for a Grenadier regiment, 5 January 1798.

(189) Pouches preserved in HIS IMPERIAL HIGHNESS GRAND DUKE MICHAEL PAVLOVICH's Own Arsenal, and HIGHEST confirmed table of uniforms, accouterments, and weaponry for a Grenadier regiment, 5 January 1798.

(190) Military Regulation of 29 November 1796, Part Ten, Chapter IV, § 6; HIGHEST confirmed table of uniforms, accouterments, and weaponry for a Grenadier regiment, 5 January 1798, and statements by contemporaries.

(191) Knapsack, flask, and rusk bag preserved in HIS IMPERIAL HIGHNESS GRAND DUKE MICHAEL PAVLOVICH's Own Arsenal; Military Regulation of 29 November 1796, Part Ten, Chapter V, § 17; HIGHEST confirmed table of uniforms, accouterments, and weaponry for a Grenadier regiment, 5 January 1798, and statements by contemporaries.

(192) Ditto.

(193) Ditto.

(194) Ditto.

(195) Ditto.

(196) Non-commissioned officers' coats preserved in HIS IMPERIAL HIGHNESS GRAND DUKE MICHAEL PAVLOVICH'S Own Arsenal; Military Regulation of 29 November 1796, Part Ten, Chapter V, §§ 3 and 11, and Chapter VI, note to § 6; HIGHEST confirmed table of uniforms, accouterments, and weaponry for a Grenadier regiment, 5 January 1798, and statements by contemporaries.

(197) Military Regulation of 29 November 1796, Part Ten, Chapter VI, § 8; HIGHEST confirmed table of uniforms, accouterments, and weaponry for a Grenadier regiment, 5 January 1798.

(198) Drummers' coats preserved in the Commissariat Department of the War Ministry and in HIS IMPERIAL HIGHNESS GRAND DUKE MICHAEL PAVLOVICH'sOwn Arsenal; Military Regulation of 29 November 1796, Part Ten, Chapter V, § 9, and Chapter VI, note to § 8; pattern drum in the Commissariat Department of the War Ministry; HIGHEST confirmed table of uniforms, accouterments, and weaponry for a Grenadier regiment, 5 January 1798; contemporary drawings and statements by contemporaries.

(199) Ditto.

(200) Ditto.

(201) Statements by contemporaries.

(202) HIGHEST confirmed table of uniforms, accouterments, and weaponry for a Grenadier regiment, 5 January 1798.

(203) Grenadier caps preserved in the Commissariat Department, the St.-Petersburg Arsenal, and HIS IMPERIAL HIGHNESS GRAND DUKE MICHAEL PAVLOVICH'sOwn Arsenal; Military Regulation of 29 November 1796, Part Ten, Chapter V, § 17, HIGHEST confirmed table of uniforms, accouterments, and weaponry for a Grenadier regiment, 5 January 1798

(204) The same table; contemporary drawings and statements from contemporaries.

(205) Ditto.

(206) Ditto.

(207) The same information as well as the Military Regulation of 29 November 1796, Part Ten, Chapter V, § 10.

(208) Musicians' coats preserved in HIS IMPERIAL HIGHNESS GRAND DUKE MICHAEL PAVLOVICH'sOwn Arsenal; Military Regulation of 29 November 1796, Part Ten, Chapter V, § 9; HIGHEST confirmed table of uniforms, accouterments, and weaponry for a Grenadier regiment, 5 January 1798; statements by contemporaries.

(209) Officers' coats preserved in HIS IMPERIAL HIGHNESS GRAND DUKE MICHAEL PAVLOVICH'sOwn Arsenal; drawings located in HIS IMPERIAL MAJESTY'S Own Library under No. 177; Military Regulation of 29

November 1796, Part Ten, Chapter IV; statements by contemporaries.

(210) Ditto.

(211) Ditto.

(212) Ditto.

(213) Swords preserved in the St.-Petersburg Arsenal and HIS IMPERIAL HIGHNESS GRAND DUKE MICHAEL PAVLOVICH'sOwn Arsenal; contemporary drawings, including those in HIS IMPERIAL MAJESTY'S Own Library under No. 177; and statements from contemporaries.

(214) The same information as referenced in the preceding note.

(215) Ditto.

(216) The same information, as well as actual spontoons preserved in the above-mentioned Arsenals and HIS IMPERIAL MAJESTY'S Own Arsenal in the Anichkov Palace.

(217) Ditto.

(218) Statements by contemporaries.

(219) Statements by contemporaries and the Military Regulation of 29 November 1796, Part Ten, Chapter IV; note to § 5.

(220) Statements by contemporaries; contemporary portraits, and a HIGHEST Order of 26 November 1796.

(221) Statements by contemporaries; and the Military Regulation of 29 November 1796, Part Ten, Chapter IV; note to § 5.

(222) Statements by contemporaries.

(223) Uniforms of lower noncombatant ranks preserved in the Commissariat Department of the War Ministry and HIS IMPERIAL HIGHNESS GRAND DUKE MICHAEL PAVLOVICH'sOwn Arsenal; HIGHEST confirmed table of uniforms, accouterments, and weaponry for a Grenadier regiment, 5 January 1798; statements by contemporaries.

(224) Ditto.

(225) Ditto.

(226) Ditto.

(227) Military Regulation of 29 November 1796, Part Ten, Chapter IV; note to § 4, and statements by contemporaries

(228) *Chronicle of the Russian Imperial Army*, compiled by Prince Dolgorukov, Nos. 10, 11, 12, 13, 15, 16, 17, 18, and 20, and these same numbered drawings located in HIS IMPERIAL MAJESTY'S Own Library under No. 177.

(229) Ditto.

(230) Ditto.

(231) Ditto.

(232) Ditto.

(223) Ditto.

(234) Ditto.

(235) Ditto.

(236) Ditto.

(237) Ibid., No. 14.

(238) Ibid., No. 19, and a fusilier cap of the Taurica Grenadier Regiment preserved in HIS IMPERIAL HIGHNESS GRAND DUKE MICHAEL PAVLOVICH'sOwn Arsenal.

(239) Ibid., No. 9, and a cap plate preserved in the Commissariat Department of the War Ministry.

(240) Ibid., No. 8, and an actual coat preserved in HIS IMPERIAL HIGHNESS GRAND DUKE MICHAEL PAVLOVICH'S Own Arsenal.

(241) HIGHEST confirmed table of uniforms, accouterments, and weaponry for a Grenadier regiment, 5 January 1798.

(242) Ditto.

(243) Ditto.

(244) Ditto.

(245) Ditto.

(246) Ditto.

(247) Ditto.

(248) The same table; *Chronicle of the Russian Imperial Army*, compiled by Prince Dolgorukov, and drawings located in HIS IMPERIAL MAJESTY'S Own Library under No. 177, Nos. 8-20.

(249)) Complete Collection of Laws of the Russian Empire (*Polnoe Sobranie Zakonov Rossiiskoi Imperii*, hereafter PSZ), Vol. XXIV, No 18,837, pg. 548, and statements by contemporaries.

(250) PSZ, Vol. XLIV, Part II, Sect. Four, in information on uniforms page 3, No. 19,178, and statements by contemporaries.

(251) HIGHEST Order.

(252) Various uniform items preserved in the Commissariat Department of the War Ministry and HIS IMPERIAL HIGHNESS GRAND DUKE MICHAEL PAVLOVICH's Own Arsenal; Military Regulation of 29 November 1796, Part Ten, Chapters II, III, IV, V, and VI; *Chronicle of the Russian Imperial Army*, compiled by Prince Dolgorukov; drawings in HIS IMPERIAL MAJESTY'S Own Library under No. 177; HIGHEST confirmed table of uniforms, accouterments, and weaponry for a Musketeer regiment, 5 January 1798; statements by contemporaries.

(253) Ditto.

(254) Ditto.

(255) Ditto.

(256) Ditto.

(257) Ditto.

(258) *Chronicle of the Russian Imperial Army*, compiled by Prince Dolgorukov, Nos. 21-82, and the same numbered drawings located in HIS IMPERIAL MAJESTY'S Own Library under No. 177.

(259) Ditto.

(260) Ditto.

(261) Ditto.

(262) Ditto.

(263) Ditto.

(264) Ditto.

(265) Ditto.

(266) Ditto.

(267) Ditto.

(268) Ditto.

(263) Ditto.

(269) Ditto.

(270) Ditto.

(271) Ditto.

(272) Ditto.

(273) Ditto.

(274) Ditto.

(275) Ditto.

(276) Ditto.

(277) Ditto.

(278) Ditto.

(279) Ditto.

(280) Ditto.

(281) Ditto.

(282) Ditto.

(283) Ditto.
(284) Ditto.
(285) Ditto.
(286) Ditto.
(287) Ditto.
(288) Ditto.
(289) Ditto.
(290) Ditto.
(291) Ditto.
(292) Ditto.
(293) Ditto.
(294) Ditto.
(295) Ditto.
(296) Ditto.
(297) Ditto.
(298) Ditto.
(299) Ditto.
(300) Ditto.
(301) Ditto.
(302) Ditto.
(303) Ditto.
(304) Ditto.
(305) Ditto.
(306) Ditto.
(307) Ditto.
(308) Ditto.
(309) Ditto.
(310) Ditto.
(311) Ditto.
(312) Ditto.
(313) Ditto.
(314) Ditto.
(315) Ditto.
(316) Ditto.
(317) Ditto.
(318) Ditto.
(319) Ditto.
(320) HIGHEST confirmed table of uniforms, accouterments, and weaponry for a Musketeer regiment, 5 January 1798.
(321) Ditto.
(322) Ditto.
(323) Ditto.
(324) Ditto.
(325) Ditto.
(326) *Chronicle of the Russian Imperial Army*, compiled by Prince Dolgorukov, Nos. 21-82, and these same numbered drawings located in HIS IMPERIAL MAJESTY'S Own Library under No. 177.
(327) Ibid., Nos. 83-88.
(328) Ditto.

(329) Ditto.

(330) Ditto.

(331) Ditto.

(332) Ditto.

(333) PSZ, Vol. XXIV, No. 18,837, pg. 548, and statements by contemporaries.

(334) PSZ, Vol. XLIV, Part II, Sect. Four, under information for uniforms, page 3, No. 19,178, and statements by contemporaries.

(335) *Chronicle of the Russian Imperial Army*, compiled by Prince Dolgorukov, No. 159; this same numbered drawing in HIS IMPERIAL MAJESTY'S Own Library under No. 177, and PSZ, Vol. XLIII, Part I, Section 1, pg. 69, No. 18,893, and pg. 138, No. 19,450.

(336) HIGHEST Order.

(337) HIGHEST confirmed table of uniforms, accouterments, and weaponry for a Jäger regiment, 5 January 1798; Chronicle of the Russian Imperial Army, compiled by Prince Dolgorukov; drawings in HIS IMPERIAL MAJESTY'S Own Library under No. 177, and statements by contemporaries.

(338) Ditto.

(339) Ditto.

(340) Ditto.

(341) Ditto.

(342) Ditto.

(343) Ditto.

(344) Ditto.

(345) Ditto.

(346) *Chronicle of the Russian Imperial Army*, compiled by Prince Dolgorukov, Nos. 226-245, and these same numbered drawing in HIS IMPERIAL MAJESTY'S Own Library under No. 177.

(347) PSZ, Vol. XXIV, No. 18,173, pg. 754.

(348) HIGHEST confirmed table of uniforms, accouterments, and weaponry for a Jäger regiment, 5 January 1798, and statements by contemporaries.

(349) Ditto.

(350) PSZ, Vol. XXIV, Part II, Sect. Four, under information for uniforms, page 3, No. 19,178, and statements by contemporaries.

(351) HIGHEST Order.

РИСУНКИ
Одежды и Вооруженія
РОССІЙСКИХЪ
ВОЙСКЪ.

PLATES LIST OF ILLUSTRATIONS

998. General. Brant's Musketeer Regiment, 1798-1801.

999. Grenadier. Müller's Musketeer Regiment, 1798-1801.

1000. Non-commissioned Officer. Marklov's Musketeer Regiment, 1798-1801.

1001. Grenadier Drummer and Company-Grade Officer. Berg's Musketeer Regiment, 1798-1801.

1002. Musician, Grenadier, and Field-grade Officer. Senate Regiment, 1800-1801.

1003. Private. 1st Jäger Regiment, 1797-1800.

1004. Non-commissioned Officer. 2nd Jäger Regiment, 1797-1801.

1005. Waldhornist. 3rd Jäger Regiment, 1797-1801.

1006. Staff-Waldhornist. 4th Jäger Regiment, 1797-1801.

1007. Officer. 5th Jäger Regiment, 1797-1801.

1008. Adjutant. 6th Jäger Regiment, 1797-1801.

1009. General. 7th Jäger Regiment, 1797-1801.

1010. Private. 8th Jäger Regiment, 1797-1801.

1011. Privates. 9th and 10th Jäger Regiments, 1797-1801.

1012. Non-commissioned Officers. 11th and 12th Jäger Regiments, 1797-1801.

1013. Non-commissioned Officers. 13th and 14th Jäger Regiments, 1797-1801.

1014. Privates. 15th and 16th Jäger Regiments, 1797-1801.

1015. Officers. 17th and 18th Jäger Regiments, 1797-1801.

1016. Wagon Masters. 19th and 20th Jäger Regiments, 1797-1801.

The first part of original volume 7 are in the our 1st volume SWU-006 Soldiershop.

Grenadier, Pskov Musketeer Regiment. Grenadier Non-commissioned Officer,
Tambov Musketeer Regiment. 1797-1801.

Field-grade Officer and Grenadier. Rostov Musketeer Regiment, 1797-1801.

Musketeer. Murom Musketeer Regiment, 1797-1801.

Field-grade Officer and Grenadier. Staryi-Oskol Musketeer Regiment, 1797-1801.

Grenadier Drummer. Tobolsk Musketeer Regiment, 1797-1801.

Grenadier Non-commissioned Officer and General. Tiflis Musketeer Regiment, 1797-1801.

Состав. Василченко и Солнцев.

Рис на кам. Белоусов и Гурке

Musician. Voronezh Musketeer Regiment, 1797-1801.

Company-grade Officer. Kazan Musketeer Regiment, 1797-1801.

Grenadier. Moscow Musketeer Regiment, 1797-1801.

Officer and Grenadier Drummer. Kabarda Musketeer Regiment, 1797-1801.

Grenadier and Officer. Vladimir Musketeer Regiment, 1797-1801.

Musketeer Non-commissioned Officer. Uglich Musketeer Regiment, 1797-1801.

Musketeer. Sevsk Musketeer Regiment, 1797-1801.

Company-grade Officer and Private. Narva Musketeer Regiment, 1797-1801.

Musketeer Non-commissioned Officer. Dnieper Musketeer Regiment, 1797-1801.

Adjutant and Musketeer. Vyatka Musketeer Regiment, 1797-1801.

Составл. Василченко и Борисовъ.   Рис. на кам. Бѣлоусовъ и Фрименрихъ.

Company-grade Officer and Private. Suzdal Musketeer Regiment, 1797-1801.

Fifer. Kexholm Musketeer Regiment, 1797-1801.

Grenadier Drummer. Viborg Musketeer Regiment, 1797-1801.

Grenadier and Field-grade Officer. Ryazan Musketeer Regiment, 1797-1801.

ЭВ 4.

Non-commissioned Officer. Neva Musketeer Regiment, 1797-1801.

Grenadier Drummer and Field-grade Officer. Sofiya Musketeer Regiment, 1797-1801.

Grenadier and Company-grade Officer. Shirvan Musketeer Regiment, 1797-1801.

Составл. Васильченко и Клюквинъ.

Рис. на кам. Бѣлоусовъ и Андерсонъ.

Grenadier Non-commissioned Officer. Perm Musketeer Regiment, 1797-1801.

988.

Drummer and Non-commissioned Officer. Nizovsk Musketeer Regiment, 1797-1801.

Non-commissioned Officer. Butyrsk Musketeer Regiment, 1797-1801.

Grenadier Non-commissioned Officer. Ufa Musketeer Regiment, 1797-1801.

Grenadier Drummer and Field-grade Officer. Rylsk Musketeer Regiment, 1797-1801.

Officer and Non-commissioned Officer. Yekaterinburg Musketeer Regiment, 1797-1801.

Grenadier Drummer and Fifer. Selenginsk Musketeer Regiment, 1797-1801.

Field-grade Officer, Musketeer, and Grenadier Drummer. Tomsk Musketeer Reg. 1797-1801.

Grenadier Non-commissioned Officer. Arkharov's Musketeer Regiment, 1797-1801.

Pioneer and Wagon Master. Pavlutskii's Musketeer Regiment, 1798-1801.

997.

Grenadier. Leitner's Musketeer Regiment, 1798-1801.

General. Brant's Musketeer Regiment, 1798-1801.

999.

Grenadier. Müller's Musketeer Regiment, 1798-1801.

Non-commissioned Officer. Marklov's Musketeer Regiment, 1798-1801.

1001.

Grenadier Drummer and Company-Grade Officer. Berg's Musketeer Regiment, 1798-1801.

Musician, Grenadier, and Field-grade Officer. Senate Regiment, 1800-1801.

Private. 1st Jäger Regiment, 1797-1800.

1004.

Составл. Васильченко и Губаревъ. Рис. на кам. Бѣлоусовъ и Андерсонъ.

Non-commissioned Officer. 2nd Jäger Regiment, 1797-1801.

Waldhornist. 3rd Jäger Regiment, 1797-1801.

Staff-Waldhornist. 4th Jäger Regiment, 1797-1801.

Officer. 5th Jäger Regiment, 1797-1801.

Adjutant. 6th Jäger Regiment, 1797-1801.

General. 7th Jäger Regiment, 1797-1801.

Private. 8th Jäger Regiment, 1797-1801.

1011.

Privates. 9th and 10th Jäger Regiments, 1797-1801.

Non-commissioned Officers. 11th and 12th Jäger Regiments, 1797-1801.

Non-commissioned Officers. 13th and 14th Jäger Regiments, 1797-1801.

Privates. 15th and 16th Jäger Regiments, 1797-1801.

Officers. 17th and 18th Jäger Regiments, 1797-1801.

Wagon Masters. 19th and 20th Jäger Regiments, 1797-1801.

WORK PLAN

Our reprint in based on the original 19th century volumes, to be precise the volumes from 7 to 9 are dedicated to the reign of Paul I; this first part is distributed on 7 volumes, having a numbering from 1 to 7. From number 10 to 18 of the original volumes, the second part is dedicated to the Russian troops under Alexander I. These still being worked on and they will be soon ready, distributed on twenty volumes approximately. Our new edition, the first ever published in English, both on paper and digital format, boasts a large number of color plates, many of them unpublished and coloured by our team of expert artists and scholars of uniformology. Each volume is based on 50/70 plates, always accompanied by the original translated text which describes the uniforms, the organization and the armament of the Russian army of the period.

 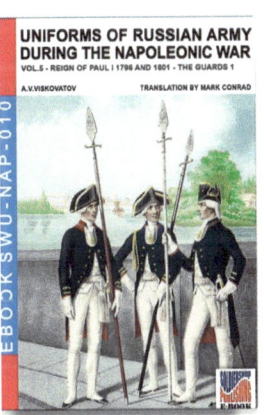  

www.ingramcontent.com/pod-product-compliance
Lightning Source LLC
Chambersburg PA
CBHW041456120626
46547CB00003B/456